DOG TRAINING
DIARIES

PROVEN EXPERT TIPS & TRICKS
TO LIVE IN HARMONY WITH YOUR DOG

TOM SHELBY

Skyhorse Publishing

Skyhorse Publishing books may be purchased in bulk at special discounts for sales promotion, corporate gifts, fund-raising, or educational purposes. Special editions can also be created to specifications. For details, contact the Special Sales Department, Skyhorse Publishing, 307 West 36th Street, 11th Floor, New York, NY 10018 or info@skyhorsepublishing.com.

Skyhorse® and Skyhorse Publishing® are registered trademarks of Skyhorse Publishing, Inc.®, a Delaware corporation.

Visit our website at www.skyhorsepublishing.com.

10 9 8 7 6 5 4 3 2 1

Library of Congress Cataloging-in-Publication Data is available on file.

Cover design by Jenny Zemanek
Cover photographs by Tom Shelby and iStockphoto

Print ISBN: 978-1-5107-3731-0
Ebook ISBN: 978-1-5107-3732-7

Printed in the United States of America

CONTENTS

INTRODUCTION

I've been a dog trainer for forty years in New York City and Martha's Vineyard. I've trained and worked with two search and rescue dogs over a twenty-year span to find missing people. Every year, I have about 800 dog-training appointments carried out in all types of dog owners' homes, from trailers outside of New York City to brownstones on the Upper West Side. The rich and famous (or RAFs as I fondly call them) also hale me out to their rural mansions. The life of the seriously RAF is something the great majority of us can only imagine, but it didn't take long for me to realize down to my core that regardless of fame or circumstances, dog owners are alike in many ways: they love their dogs, they do stupid things that cause problems with their dogs, and they need as much training and sometimes more than their dogs.

I had humble beginnings. I got my big break in the dog training business when I got a job with an outfit that rented and sold attack dogs in Brooklyn. I managed to get hired because I was the first person who was able to con a trained attack dog into letting me pet him. After that, I moved on to training the dogs of actors, celebrities, athletes, and even pimps. When each door opens, I assess both dog and owner, their relationship, and their environment. When it comes to dogs and people, it's not about the money, it's about the relationship.

I don't whisper. I don't yell. I am an "it depends" trainer. I use a variety of techniques gleaned through my many years of practice to get dogs to cooperate with their owners. Dogs are adorable, wonderful, mischievous, afraid, and more often than not wildly out of control. The truth is, it usually only takes me a few minutes to train the dogs but a lot longer to train their owners. At $265 an hour, one wife of a Mafioso told me I was more expensive than her shrink. I replied, "Yes, but I'm getting results."

When it's dog-related, I rarely see or hear something I haven't seen or heard a million times. In this book, I'm going to give you tips, advice, strategies, and insight for how to deal with the most common problematic situations my clients face. I'll be answering real questions from real dog owners to give you a better understanding of the typical reasons for your dog's behavior and concrete steps you can take to live in harmony with your four-legged significant other. By reading this book, you will learn how to harmonize with your dog, understand them, teach them, and also learn from them. Because that's what it's all about—harmony between dog and family.

I've organized the book so that it can be read in any order you prefer. As you read the different chapters, you will notice that certain strategies are repeated and that in some cases I refer you to other chapters for more in-depth information on key training concepts and methods. This is intentional. Over the course of my training career, I've learned that many of these strategies can be applied successfully to a variety of situations.

PART 1

HOUSEBREAKING

Dogs have "den instinct." I think people do, too. That's why we love the comfort and security of our home, be it a house or apartment. The house is our den and the bedroom is what I refer to as our "inner den." When we really feel lousy or sick, we go to bed, to our inner den. You want your dog to see the house as his den and his crate as his inner den. Used properly, the crate is invaluable for housebreaking and preventing unwanted behaviors, such as chewing shoes or chairs and urinating or defecating in the house.

CHAPTER 1

HOW DO I TEACH MY PUPPY NOT TO PEE AND POOP IN THE HOUSE?

Dogs have a "den instinct," the den being where they eat and sleep. Wolf puppies leave the dugout in the ground to relieve themselves, and then return to the den to eat and sleep. The farm dog that lives in the barn or doghouse doesn't pee there and lie in it. Those few that do lie in their own excrement forged the expression "dirty dog." Aside from those occasional exceptions, dogs don't like to make where they eat and sleep, just as we don't have meals in the bathroom. So, the key to prevent peeing and pooping in the home is to stimulate and sustain the den instinct.

Initially, most mothers will clean up after their pups. Dogs are strong creatures of habit, and what they're standing on when they first become cognizant of the comfort of relieving themselves can be meaningful. That's been my experience. Getting a puppy accustomed as soon as possible to relieving himself outdoors, instead of on floors and carpets, can speed up the housebreaking process. If there have already been some accidents, try to neutralize the odor of the mistakes, because your dog will be tempted to urinate or defecate where he smells them. White vinegar is cheap and effective for that.

First things first: teach your dog to love his crate and see it as his inner den. This is where we ignite the den instinct. The crate will be a sanctuary, never a place of punishment.

Step 1: Place the crate in a confined area, using a gate or X-pen (an eight-paneled metal gate with all panels jointed so it can be easily configured any way you want).

Step 2: Stay with the same command word or words: "Go to your house," "bed," "place," "incarceration"—whatever! Give him vocabulary.

Step 3: Put his bed in the crate and toss treats to lure him in without closing the door. You want to create a very positive association with the crate. Whenever he is in there, praise him lavishly and boisterously. Toss lots of small treats, so they seem to be coming in from every angle (above, sides, front, back). Being in the crate should be great fun.

Step 4: Feed him his meals in the crate by putting his bowl inside and leaving the door open. Do not lock him in at this point.

When he's going in on his own and you feel the time is right, which can be a lot sooner than you may think, close the door. Do it with love and with people-food treats. Maybe put in a hollow marrow bone with a piece of chicken wedged in the middle when you close the door. Open the door after a few minutes and just step back saying nothing. He just might keep "hanging in" instead of "running out." With success building on success, increase the confinement time. If he complains and wants out, bang on the crate lightly, say "Uh-UH," and walk away. Only let him out when he's not complaining. Your pup should spend the night sleeping in his inner den.

Whenever he's not with you or can't be observed, he's confined in his den area with love and treats. Period. No exceptions. There can be no exceptions, because every time he relieves himself in the house, that behavior becomes more habitual. Be preventative—like potty training a kid, only your puppy will probably be a lot easier to train than my two-year-old grandson.

If your pup's eating times are reasonably consistent, you'll get a quick handle on when he has to make in relation to when he eats. Feed him on a structured basis with three meals a day until he's about sixteen weeks old, then twice a day. Lose the middle meal. He's got about twenty minutes to eat, or he misses the meal. Cut the water off by 6:30 p.m. so your pup has a better chance of holding it all night sooner. A dog needs one cup of water for every eight pounds of weight in a twenty-four-hour period to be properly hydrated. Most vets will tell you to have water always available because they've had clients actually dehydrating their dogs by holding water back to eliminate the peeing mistakes. However, many dogs will drink out of boredom, which is why I recommend not making water available at night. If he keeps going to water bowl, give him an ice cube to wet his whistle as opposed to filling his bladder.

During the day, toss special treats in the crate and praise him whenever he goes in, making sure it's the most physically comfortable place for him to hang out. Keep an eye on him and take him outside to relieve himself when he indicates the need. Signs of a dog seriously needing to go are a sudden intense sniffing (looking for the right place to pee) or a kind of darting back and forth or circling (looking for the right place to poop). Praise your puppy with voice and treat as soon as he's finished eliminating in the right place, in other words, outside. The timing here is critical so that he relates the treats and praise to having done the right thing in the right place.

During the night, your pup is in his den. There are two ways to handle the night hours. You can place a wee-wee pad off to the side of the crate that is boxed in by an X-pen. Before you place the pad down, just touch one of his poops or some pee along its surface. The smell will likely lure him to the pad to do his business. Keep the crate door open so he can easily exit and reenter, keeping his inner den clean.

If you don't want a pee pad in the house and have easy access to an outdoor space, place the crate near your bed with the crate door closed. When you hear your pup crying or whimpering, in other words telling you "I gotta go!" fly out of bed and get him outside immediately. When outside, the instant he finishes relieving himself, praise him quietly. Keep the praise low-key so he goes back to sleep.

Most dogs have the ability to hold it all night when they are about ten weeks old.

Remember when indoors, if your puppy is not in the crate, he should be supervised. Period. If he can't be watched, he should be in the crate with good toys. Every time he has a mistake, it's a half-step backward. The final goal is to expand the den from his crate to the whole house so that he only relieves himself outdoors.

CHAPTER 2

HOW DO I TEACH MY OLDER DOG NOT TO PEE AND POOP IN THE HOUSE?

Even if your dog loads the dishwasher, takes out the garbage, and does your kid's homework, if he still poops or pees in the house, it's no good! When I was training full-time in New York, I met a Rottweiler named Donna that was relegated to a crate outside in the yard because she was so dirty. This was a nice dog that you didn't want to pet or even touch because her whole body was constantly covered with caked-on feces. The owners, however, were not clueless about dogs or Rottys. While Dirty Donna lived outside, their other Rottweiller, Bobby, lived inside, no problem. When I was asked why, after twenty-five years of owning Rottys with no problems, Donna would make in the crate and lie in it, my answer was, "weak to nonexistent den instinct."

For an older dog, you will need to revive the dormant "den" instinct. Dogs don't like to eat where they make, just like us two-leggeds don't like to have our meals in the bathroom. After peeing anytime, anyplace, your dog may just believe that the whole world is his personal urinal. We're not talking about clueless puppies who have no concept of "holding it in" until the location for "letting it go" is right. Your dog needs an epiphany, that moment of realization that he, Emperor Dog, is a clean emperor who would never pee where he eats or sleeps. If there have already been some accidents, or probably not-accidents, you need to try to neutralize the odor of the pee and poop spots, because your dog will be attracted to urinate or defecate where he smells them. Use white vinegar or a comparable product.

The first order of business is teaching your dog to love his crate and see it as his inner den. This is where we rekindle the den instinct. The crate should be his sanctuary, never a punishment. Your dog should love his crate because that's where the best things happen!

Step 1: Get a crate large enough for your dog to stretch out lying down, but not so large that he can pee in one end and get away from it at the other end. Put his favorite bed in the crate ("den").

Step 2: Use the same word or words every time you send him to the crate while teaching him to keep his den clean. Some good ones are: "Go home," "bed," "place," whatever! Give him vocabulary.

Step 3: Toss treats to lure him in without closing the door. You want to create a very positive association with the crate. Whenever he is in there, praise him lavishly and boisterously. Toss lots of small treats so they seem to be coming in from every angle (above, sides, front, back). Be playful. Being in the crate should be fun.

Step 4: Feed him his meals in the crate, putting his bowl inside and leaving the door open. Do not lock him in yet. When not having meals, put his favorite cushions in the crate.

Once your dog is going in the crate on his own, it's time to close the door and contain him for short periods of time. Do it with love and with people-food treats. Maybe put in a hollow marrow bone with a piece of chicken wedged in the middle when you close the door. Open the door after a few minutes and just step back saying nothing. He just might keep "hanging in" instead of "running out." With success building on success, increase the confinement time. If he complains and wants out, bang on the crate lightly, say "Uh-UH," and walk away. Only let him out when he's not complaining. Your dog should spend the night sleeping in his den. Whenever he's not with you or can't be observed, he should be confined in his den with love and treats. Period. No exceptions.

When your dog is not in the crate, he should be observed by you and dragging a flat leash (with the handle cut off so it's less likely to get caught on things as the dog is moving around the house). He may not know he is being observed, but you will never lose him from your line of sight even if you have to use a mirror (because dogs get very good at being sneaky). No ifs, ands, or buts. What happens in most cases all over the world is that an owner sees his dog start to relieve himself indoors and goes charging at him, arms flailing, yelling whatever he's yelling, to stop him from eliminating. And what does the dog learn from this? Well, from the dog's perspective, when you see him urinating or defecating, you clearly lose your mind. So, they wait until you're distracted and then step out of sight behind the couch and take a quick pee to avoid your insane reaction to their natural needs. Don't worry, though. Sneaky Boots will not have the ability to slip out of sight to pee or poop without being caught and stopped by the Dog God.

The Dog God is anything that startles your dog. The Dog God sees all, all the time, and does not like dogs to relieve themselves inside the home. The Dog God cannot be connected with you and has nothing to do with you. Strategically place several empty soda or beer cans filled with a dozen pennies around the house so you can quickly and stealthily pick them up. As soon as your dog starts to go, shake the can or throw it near him (depending on your dog's sensitivity). Hopefully that stops the elimination process. You can also wear a whistle around your neck and blast it if he starts to pee or poop. Again, make sure you're not seen as the whistleblower. If you're successful, he will jump a couple of feet in the air instead of relieving himself, at which point you calmly pick up the leash he's been dragging and take him outside. After he's taken care of business in the correct location, and only then, reward him with praise and a treat.

I'd also suggest that you feed your older dog a couple of times a week right on the spots where he urinated or defecated in the house, further incorporating those areas as living areas instead of toilets. When he is accident-free for a month, you can start leaving him out of the crate without supervision for short periods. Increase the unsupervised time slowly, with success building on success.

DOG TRAINING DIARY

JOAN RIVERS AND THE DOG GOD

> "Creativity is just connecting things."
> —Steve Jobs, *Washington Post*

Joan's penthouse triplex off 5th Avenue reminded me of Versailles the moment I walked in. The Versailles vibe was not because the decor was too ostentatious, opulent, or overdone. Like Versailles, there was a lot of gold and silver and crystal, and the couches and settees were matching, colorful, and plush, but it all worked! The artwork was eclectic and engaging and the whole place just seemed inviting and beautiful.

I wanted to say that I loved the interior decorating but didn't want to sound like I was sucking up to her; however, before I could get beyond initial greetings I was accosted by Sam, the six-month-old Havanese puppy, and Max, the seven-year-old Pekingese. I was there for Sam, who thought the whole world was his urinal, Versailles included. Getting a comedian to laugh, especially when they're paying you, is not an easy thing to do. But I actually got her to crack a smile when I said with some

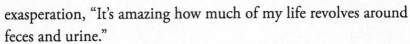

exasperation, "It's amazing how much of my life revolves around feces and urine."

The key "help" were instrumental in following through with my instruction. There was Jocelyn, who had called me at the vet's suggestion, and husband and wife Kevin and Debbie, who lived downstairs. Most of the RAF (Rich and Famous) just want to cuddle and play with their already-trained dogs and leave the mundane details of training—housebreaking, destructive chewing, jumping, separation anxiety, etc.—to the assistants, which can undermine the training to some extent because of the lack of consistency. In this case, it basically fell on Kevin's and Debbie's shoulders. They were very responsive, which is usually the case with RAF helpers who want to continue working for the RAF. This is not often the case with many non-RAF nannies, au pairs, and assistants when a new puppy is brought into a home. With a nanny who's been there for years, the response is typically "Training a dog is not part of my job description! I'm not adding multiple dog walks and cleaning puppy diarrhea to my already hectic schedule."

So, for the millionth time, I walked everyone through a dog's den instinct (using a crate properly), proper feeding and walking schedules, the importance of removing the scent of urine and fecal mishaps, how *not* to correct the dog, and the concept of the Dog God.

Joan was politely pretending to listen to most of what I was saying (figuring Kevin and Debbie would take care of the mundane stuff), but she perked up at the mention of the Dog God.

"Dog God?" she said. "I've never heard the rabbi, nor a priest or minister for that matter, mention the existence of a Dog God. Where is he mentioned in the Bible?"

I smiled at that. "First of all, Joan, God isn't He. She's female, including the Dog God. Just ask my wife."

I was on a roll: she smiled again and said, "Okay, tell us about this feminine deity."

"Let's say you have a well-mannered dog who wouldn't disturb you or your food while you're snacking at the coffee table in front of the TV."

"Okay," she said.

"But when you leave the room to answer the phone, the dog plunders the food-laden table. Or the dog acts like the garbage can doesn't exist in your presence but raids it the moment you leave."

Eyebrows perked, she said, "Go on, where does the Dog God fit in here?"

"Well," I continued. "The dog needs to understand that the Dog God sees all, all the time, and doesn't like it when the coffee table or garbage can is raided whether you are in the room or not."

Getting a little frustrated now, Joan said, "Really! And how does the Dog God tell my Sammy to leave my food alone when no one's in the room, which, by the way, is a real issue with the little stinker. She doesn't even wait till I'm out of the room before she's grabbing what she can."

"The Dog God, as one would suspect, can take many forms. In this case she would take the form of an empty soda can or beer can with a dozen pennies in it with Scotch tape over the top so the pennies can't fall out. Next comes the entrapment. We set Sammy up with a hot dog in a very perforated plastic container on the coffee table and leave the room. However, there's a mirror set up so you can see the table even though you're outside the room. The second Sammy so much as sniffs the container with the hot dog, the can with the pennies flies into the room near her. Sammy will startle herself through the ceiling, but she will relate the shock of the noise to taking the food, not to you. You say nothing, you had nothing to do with it. It's the Dog God who doesn't like it when Sammy pilfers from the coffee table, and she throws noisy cans."

This brought another smile, but then she said, "So, how does this relate to housebreaking?"

"Well, think about it, Joan. What do people all over the world do when they see their puppy starting to urinate in the house?" Before she could say anything, I went on: "They're charging at the dog with their arms flailing, yelling whatever they're yelling to stop the dog from peeing. And what does the puppy learn from this? She learns that she can't make with you looking. She's just doing what comes naturally, peeing when she has to, and from her point of view, when you see her doing it, you lose your mind by charging at her yelling with your arms flailing. So, puppies quickly learn, all over the world, to become sneaky about it. They wait till the phone rings, something distracts you, then they sneak behind the couch, take a quick pee, then quickly return with a 'Hey, how's it going?' Hoping you missed it."

As is usually the case, heads were nodding when I said this. Debbie immediately piped in. "Sam never gets caught. She always seems to make in the one instant I'm busy with something else. As hard as I try to pay attention, she always makes in the one moment I can't attend to her!"

"It's not a coincidence, Debbie," I explained. "She may actually have held it for some time just waiting for you to look away. As I tell people all the time, dogs are smarter than you think. They get away with what they can and are very manipulative."

"I'll be damned," was her response.

I gestured toward the X-pen, an eight-paneled jointed gate that I told them to get ahead of time. "So," I said. "You will use the gate to keep Sam confined in whatever area you're in and always have a Dog God (throw can) within reach. If you see her sniffing intently she's probably looking for a place to pee. Be ready to shake or throw the can and stop her without her seeing you do it. Then, take her out, and as soon as she's done her business, praise her and give her a treat. Consistent feeding and walking times will give you a good idea of her 'need to go out' times."

I reminded them of the importance of eliminating the smell of her mistakes. "She can smell a bone fifty feet under the water of a rowboat," I said. "All I'd have to teach her is to tell me when she does. Every dog is very attracted to pee where they smell pee stains. Blot it up, then use white vinegar or one of the commercial odor neutralizers. Whatever you do, don't use anything with ammonia in it. Uric acid has ammonia in it and it will attract her to make."

As I suspected, when it came to sit, stay, and come with an automatic sit, Sam was a quick learner. The lesson ended with my most common homework assignment: "Fifteen to twenty 'comes' a day (when she doesn't expect it, call Sam to come) and have her sit when she arrives. The first four times she gets a treat after she sits, and after that she gets the treat intermittently. Intermittency is the strongest way to condition an animal (or a person, for that matter). I want her attitude to be 'Maybe there's a treat, maybe not. I'd better go check it out.' Practice it as best you can and call me with any questions. The next time I see you, you'll be working with Sam and I'll be concentrating on your body language, voice intonation, and timing."

The next lesson a week later was quite interesting. As the door opened I was literally blinded by camera lights and accosted by a microphone inches from my face. It was part of the filming of *A Year in the Life of Joan Rivers* and I just happened to be within the timeframe of that year. The whole lesson was filmed and I had to sign a release form in case I was included in the documentary. I actually thought I might be included because Joan had just come out with her own jewelry line, and being magnanimous in front of the cameras she offered me a couple of pieces as a gift to take home to my wife, Jaye. Plus, when I had her work with Sam, they did reasonably well together (thank God).

Naturally, I looked forward to the release of the documentary, but alas, I was edited out, and my daughter Kerry claimed the baubles for herself over Jaye's mild objections.

PART 2

SEPARATION ANXIETY

If you're willing to quit your job and never leave the house without your dog, then separation anxiety is not a problem for you. For the rest of us that have to go out without our four-legged friends at some point, many return to a situation that makes a strong case for DNI (Dog Needs Improvement).

CHAPTER 3

HOW DO I GO TO WORK WITHOUT COMING HOME TO A TRASHED HOUSE?

The dog with a severe separation problem that lives with a traveling salesman starts to get nervous when the suitcase is pulled out and is a basket case by the time it's packed. Your dog is totally aware of all the things you regularly do before you leave. From putting on shoes or jewelry and brushing your hair, to grabbing your cell phone or house keys, your dog knows all the things you do before you leave the house better than you do and gets more and more nervous as you get closer to walking out the door. Separation anxiety can take lots of different forms, from crying and barking, to scratching doors and screens, chewing on your shoes or table legs, and even pooping in the house. There are several things you can do to help your four-legged significant other cope better with your absence.

The very first thing I recommend is that you de-emotionalize leaving and coming. No dropping to your knees with hugs and kisses, bemoaning the time apart. Just give a pat on the head, say "See ya later, Bella," and book out. Same when you return. Pat on the head, "How ya doin', Bella," and go about your day.

You can also desensitize your dog to the nerve-racking cues that you're "splitting" on her. Go through all your cues once or twice a day, and *don't* leave. Remember, dogs are very clever, so be sure to observe yourself carefully to ensure that you perform your own personal routine. When you are actually leaving, observe the minutia of all you do before you walk out and note it in great detail, so that you don't leave anything whatsoever out when you pretend to be leaving.

The ultimate goal is to teach your dog that good things happen when you are not around. Instead of chewing on the leg of your chair, give her a more desirable alternative. The only time on planet Earth when she gets people food is when you leave her alone. As you head out, give her three or four hollow marrow bones that have people food wedged in the middle so that she really has to work at getting some of it. I'm not talking about leaving her a half a cow to munch on while you're gone, just a little meat or cheese, peanut butter—whatever she really likes. She'll appreciate it more if she has to earn it with a little work. She may not even be able to get all the people food out; that's okay. It's very important that all the bones are removed and put out of her reach or purview as soon as you get home, otherwise they will lose their specialness.

"Special toys" can also be employed to keep your dog from performing unwanted behavior during short absences. If you're going to separate for twenty minutes to take a shower or shovel the snow from the driveway, put up a gate and give your dog a couple of the special toys. There's a good chance she'll prefer them over your socks and table legs. For longer absences, interactive toys can be effective too—the type where, by knocking the toy around, it occasionally releases a treat or two. Like the hollow bones, only give your dog the special treat or toys when she's left alone, to keep the interest level high.

Another good strategy is making your departure fun. Toss five or six small regular dog treats into the room as you leave. When my five-pound dog MacDuff went blind at age eleven, he loved it when we left. I'd say, "See ya later, Duff," and throw a half-dozen treats into the living room. He probably took a good ten minutes to track them all down, and then he spent time looking in case he missed any. Then, he needed a nap!

A dog owner once told me she plays NPR for her dog so that the dog could hear human voices and intelligent programming to keep him comfortable and relaxed when home alone. NPR, with people talking, is definitely better than stone silence, but better than your dog listening to conversation is the sound of classical music, especially when played on a harpsichord. Believe it or not, country-western music works really well, too. Your dog's hearing is probably about sixteen times better than yours, so not too loud.

For the nervous dog, you may want to consider buying a ThunderShirt or Anxiety Wrap for your dog to wear whenever you leave. An Anxiety Wrap is a vest that your dog wears. A ThunderShirt uses the same principles but is made of a lighter material. There is a great deal of anecdotal evidence that the tightness of the vest seems to ground the dog and reduce some of the dog's anxiety. I've actually witnessed dogs clearly relaxing when they wore an Anxiety Vest or ThunderShirt.

The only sure way to keep your dog from destroying anything in the house or exhibiting other unwanted behavior due to separation anxiety is for a dog to be properly crate trained. That's why it's so important to have your dog see her crate as her den and love it. The crate is her sanctuary. A dog who sees her time there as a punishment might self-mutilate or hurt herself trying to chew her way out. You want to create a very positive association with the crate and make sure it's the most physically comfortable place for her to hang out. Put her bed and her favorite cushions in the crate. Toss in treats and give her special toys. Whenever she is in there, praise her lavishly and boisterously. Regardless of how comfortable your dog is in the crate, if you are going to be gone for a full work day (around twelve hours), you will need to hire a dog walker to take your dog out to relieve herself and get some exercise. No question about it. Except for overnight, I don't recommend any dog be left in a crate for more than six hours. For puppies, the timing I suggest is month(s) plus one, so if your dog is three months old, expect him to be able to hold it for a maximum of four hours. These, of course, are generalizations, as genetics vary from dog to dog. Nonetheless, they are good guidelines. I talk extensively about crating in Part 1: Housebreaking.

CHAPTER 4

HOW CAN I HELP MY DOG'S SEVERE SEPARATION ANXIETY?

Virtually every puppy will prefer your or someone else's presence rather than being alone. The anxiety of being separated can vary greatly. The normal separation nervousness can be easily addressed as the dog comes to trust that you'll always return, so doing the basics (de-emotionalizing, providing special toys, etc.) should result in problem-free separation. The more severe cases will require much more effort. Very severe cases can present diarrhea, regurgitating, self-mutilating, constant howling, and breaking teeth during escape endeavors. For those dogs with severe separation anxiety, other strategies and tools need to be employed.

Under more standard circumstances, crating your dog is pretty much a foolproof strategy, but I would not recommend it here. Often, dogs with severe separation anxiety also suffer from barrier frustration, in which case the dog becomes even more crazed at the confinement. A dog with barrier frustration literally can't handle any type of physical barrier (gate, door, fence, etc.) preventing him from going where he wants to go.

One of the most difficult cases I encountered was a young adult Yorkie whose chronic bloody footprints were sad evidence of her intense barrier frustration. Whenever left alone, she went to the apartment's front door and scratched at it until her feet bled. If left in the bedroom with the door closed, she worked at that door continually, sheer exhaustion being the only short respite until she was at it again. If Mom went into the bathroom and closed the door with Yorkie Girl on the outside, it was full-on scratching. She had the same response to a gate, crate, or barrier of any kind. There wasn't a door in the apartment that didn't need painting, and her feet were always abraded.

My first attempt was simple, straightforward, and seemingly foolproof: boots. They didn't work. They did nothing to stop the behavior as all of them came off after a couple of minutes. After several other unsuccessful attempts, I came up with a brilliant idea, I thought. Eliminate the barrier! I had building maintenance put an eye hook in the ceiling in the middle of the big living room. I then attached a somewhat elastic line from the eye hook to the floor where I placed her favorite bed, food and water bowls, and toys. Yorkie Girl then got a harness that was clipped to the elastic line. Now when left alone, she was confined without a barrier to scratch against! She could access her bed, bowls, and toys without a wall in her face to frustrate her. Yorkie Girl's owners told me I was brilliant as we stepped out of the apartment and waited on the other side of the door to see how it would go. Unbelievably, a minute later, we heard her nails on the other side of the door. Somehow, she had pulled herself out of the harness! So, I cinched the harness a lot tighter and we tried again. Long story short, we tried many different harnesses, some of which I had on so tight I was afraid she would pass out from lack of oxygen, but to no avail. She was the Houdini of harness escapes. It came down to drugs prescribed by the vet. My so-called brilliance was a depressing failure to me.

One idea to consider is a DAP (dog-appeasing pheromone) collar which can be quite relaxing for dogs. Think of this as doggy aromatherapy. My daughter uses one for her dog Kelsey. She can tell when the DAP collar is running low by the change in Kelsey's behavior. It's subtle—Kelsey's ears are cocked and her walk is more stiff-legged—but the signs are there. Her dog is clearly more relaxed with the DAP collar.

My personal preference is always to try behavior modification before resorting to medicating your dog, but extreme cases require that all routes be explored that can give you and your dog relief from a bad situation, so you shouldn't hesitate to pursue them with professional input. Any decisions must be made in close consultation with a veterinary expert. For example, Clomicalm was FDA-approved years ago for dogs suffering from separation anxiety. In my experience, it doesn't work for all dogs, and when it does, it takes about six weeks to become therapeutic. More often than not, when drugs are used, it's not a lifetime deal. Coupled with behavior modification, dosages are often lowered and the dogs are eventually weaned from them altogether.

PART 3

AGGRESSION

Of the various types of aggressive response presented by dogs, the ones I've encountered most often are: dominant aggression (Don't tell me to get off the couch! I don't want to go out now!), resource guarding/possessive aggression (Don't even think about taking away this tissue or the baby back rib that dropped on the floor), and fear aggression (Sometimes the best defense against what's making me uncomfortable is a good offense). Aggression never lessens on its own. It always gets worse until you do something to check it.

CHAPTER 5

HOW DO I STOP MY DOG FROM BARKING EVERY TIME SOMEONE WALKS PAST MY FRONT DOOR?

Adog barking is a matter of territorial aggression, and territoriality is one of the key reasons man and dog bonded thousands of years ago. It should actually be a comfort to know that when you're home with your dog, nobody can ever sneak into your house undetected. Your dog will always warn you! It's territorial instinct, and your dog's hearing is far superior to yours. This natural ability can often be valuable to us humans even outside of the home. When I was still active in search and rescue, if I was on a "high probability" search, meaning that the missing person was very possibly still alive, I used to blow a whistle and then observe my dog. If my dog cocked her ears and looked in a specific direction, perhaps the missing person had heard the whistle and responded. I couldn't hear the person, but my dog could!

Territoriality can present itself as the maniacal dog smashing itself into the car window trying to get to the gas station attendant for approaching the car. It can also be the Lab with loving eyes and tail that brings the guest a toy after a couple of barks to let its owners know somebody entered their territory, yet this super-friendly dog would probably be quite aggressive if someone were trying to climb through a window in the middle of the night. It's why you're unlikely to enter a fenced yard with a German shepherd behind the gate.

Of course, we're grateful for our dog's early warning system, but too much barking can quickly become a nuisance. Let's look at two scenarios: barking when someone approaches the door and barking when your dog sees someone passing by your property. Let's start with the door.

Your dog needs to learn to cooperate with you when you say "Quiet!" I don't want to shut down his barking when there's someone at the door, which is a completely natural instinct, but rather modify it through redirection.

Step 1: As a visitor approaches, Terrific Terrier barks to inform you, and you thank him for the warning with some praise.
Step 2: Instruct your dog to go to his spot, luring him away from the door with a treat, and have him sit and stay.
Step 3: Open the door to greet the guest, followed by releasing Terrific Terrier from his spot to come and say hello by sitting politely and getting a second treat.

While we are talking here about barking at the door, this unwanted behavior can overlap with other issues related to how your dog greets guests when they arrive. It's what I call the "door turmoil routine" which I discuss in detail in Part 4: Turmoil at the Door.

As for keeping an eye on your property as a whole, dogs will be watchful from inside your home, peering through windows or from the porch or yard. Almost all dogs love a window view when they have to remain home. Many clients over the years have complained to me that their dogs climbed onto the back of the couch so that they could see out the bay window, especially when no one was home.

Porches are also perfect lookouts, but we don't want it to cause acoustic trauma to you and your neighbors every time a person or dog happens by. My Paula and MacDuff love hanging out on my porch, as did all my dogs over the years, and there's no reason you and your dog shouldn't enjoy fresh air, a beautiful sunset, or a view of the stars from your porch, as well. For this circumstance, I recommend a two-pronged approach—and the timing is important here. When someone is going past your home, before your dog barks, start loving and praising her with your voice. Your attitude is: "Look at that! A friendly person is passing by! Isn't that great, Barky?" At the same time, offer her treats, maybe even chicken or hot dog pieces—as long as she's not barking. If the only time she gets people food is when people are passing by, she may look to you for her treat instead of yelling about it. Now, the second prong varies greatly with the sensitivity of your dog. Use the command "Quiet" when you want your dog to stop barking, accompanied with a correction that will cause the dog to stop barking, even if only for a second. The correction could be a slight tug on a leash that your dog is dragging, or the quick shake of an empty beer can with a dozen pennies in it. The moment the barking stops, you're back to praise and treats. This is where the timing is so important. If it's off, your dog may associate the correction with the presence of the passer-by and not the barking, which will exacerbate the problem.

If your dog keeps barking, a good spritz of water from a spray bottle or water pistol often works well. You're not looking to give your dog a facial, so make sure your H_2O firearm sprays a good stream, not a mist. When her mouth opens to bark, say "Quiet" firmly and spray her between the eyes a split second after the command. The moment the noise stops, praise her and, as the person passes by and Barky stays silent, give her treats. You may eventually find that you just have to reach for the bottle or pistol and she's already quieted down.

You may also discover that your dog has the sensitivity of Godzilla, in which case there are ultrasound devices that make high frequency noises that most dogs find distracting, citronella spray collars, and all kinds of shock collars to stop unwanted noise. That being said, I wouldn't consider any of these without trying behavior modification with a pro first.

CHAPTER 6

WHAT IS THE BEST WAY TO TRAIN MY DOG NOT TO CHASE OTHER ANIMALS?

Dogs, although domesticated, evolved from wolves, and are predator animals. It's why the puppy leaps after the blowing leaf, why many dogs are car chasers, and why you should never run from an aggressive dog. The fast movement elicits the prey drive! Add noise to the movement, such as a squawking chicken or a screaming child, and it intensifies the prey drive in dogs.

I remember hearing about a pony on Martha's Vineyard that was killed by a dog. Although we think of both animals as our companions, the reality is that dogs are predators and horses are prey animals. I believe it's one of the reasons horses sleep standing up, but when I toured Iceland, I noticed lots of horses lying down with only one horse standing nearby. I asked my horse-expert friend Annie about it and she told me it's because there are no predators there that horses have to worry about. She also told me it's in the nature of prey animals to look out for each other, hence the horse standing nearby guarding, just in case.

Canine predatory aggression is inherent in all dogs, but the intensity of a dog's predatory response, while mostly genetic, can vary greatly because of domestication and training. When was the last time you saw a seeing-eye dog drag his ward into traffic chasing a pigeon? Yet, I've had a ton of lessons helping Manhattan dogs that became totally wild upon seeing a squirrel. My Doberman, Michelle, would stand under our parakeet cage and whine, which was my cue to let the birds out. They loved each other! Michelle would lie down, and the birds would immediately fly down to her and climb all over her. My other Dobe, Mike, would have killed and eaten the parakeets in a heartbeat if given the chance. Terriers are bred to hunt and kill the vermin in the barn. Beagles are scent hounds. Unlike the working-group dogs whose attitude is, "Gimmie a job to do so I can please you," or the herding group's attitude, "Gimmie something to herd," the scent hound's attitude is, "I've found a scent, need to follow it, see ya!"

I've had to confront canine predatory aggression a thousand times. The base of how to address this is the "Leave it" command. In truth, my training methods can vary greatly. My approach teaching "Leave it" to a young 108-pound bullmastiff who caught and killed several woodchucks varies greatly from the approach teaching a sensitive standard poodle who wanted to kill cats, but the basic principle of "Leave it" remains the same. The "it" in "Leave it" can apply to any dog or squirrel you want your dog to ignore but can also be applied to a pizza crust on the sidewalk or your child's toy.

If your dog is going to be off leash in a place where there are possible confrontations with dogs, squirrels, coyotes, skunks, porcupines, or even cars, the "Leave it" command is critical, followed by the recall (come), and the command to stay. These three commands should be excellent in the house as a base for outdoor off-leash cooperation and fun. I discuss recall extensively in Part 6: Coming When Called, but will focus here on its application in battling a dog's natural predatory aggression. For this kind of case, my training mantra for battling canine predatory aggression is: increase the intensity of the distraction (treat) that the dog has to leave alone. Few distractions are stronger than a dog's predatory instinct.

Let's start with the command to "Come," which should be easy for you and your dog to learn. Simply call your dog to come—a lot! The first four times, he gets a treat when he arrives. Thereafter, he gets them intermittently. You want to add that bit of anticipation that keeps him coming back. "Will there be a treat? Won't there be a treat? I better check it out!" If you and I walked around Martha's Vineyard together, you would see me call my dog Paula Jean a bunch of times, and, even if she's running away from me, you'll see her flip around and come back to me for the possibility of a treat. Every time.

Teaching the "Leave it" command starts in the house, and I recommend you work with a pro if you are concerned about unwanted behavior due to predatory aggression. Typically, I begin by asking the dog owners to place a plate with meat on the floor in the middle of a room while the dog and I are in another room. I enter with the dog on his leash. Without fail, the dog heads for the plate of meat. Just before he gets to it, I say "Leave it!" immediately followed by a leash snap. The leash snap is a very quick jerk on the leash to the side, avoiding impact and pressure on the trachea. The leash must be loose, with absolutely no restraining or pulling on the leash! I also recommend that the owners place a couple of metal tags on the collar because the chinking sound of the tags adds to the surprise. As soon as your dog leaves it, he gets treats and praise. In no time flat, most dogs see the meat as something nasty, something to be ignored when they hear the words "Leave it," and instead come to me for a treat. When your dog's off-leash "Leave it" response is extremely reliable indoors, it's time to bring him outdoors, using a long line on a harness. If the lead is fastened to a collar and your dog takes off at full speed after a rabbit and the lead catches on something, it can break his neck, hence the harness.

Ideally, start in a large, fenced-in area with your dog dragging a long line attached to a harness instead of a collar. Like the plate with meat on the floor, be prepared with several things planted to tempt him so you can practice "Leave it." The temptation item needs to be large enough that your dog can't swallow it quickly. This is important because you don't want your dog to reward himself with the verboten (a.k.a. forbidden) object by eating it. The object can be a tennis ball rubbed with a piece of cheese or a huge bone, whatever. Just as your dog sniffs the object, he hears "Leave it," and gets a snap on the line if he doesn't immediately turn away from it. When he does leave it he should get lots of praise and a couple of treats when he comes back to you. If the only place on planet Earth he gets people food is outdoors and off leash when he cooperates, he'll probably cooperate quicker!

Here is where we will increase the intensity of the distraction that the dog has to leave alone, with success building on success. You want your dog to cooperate by leaving several different normally irresistible temptations, and you want to increase the value of the treat, maybe steak or lobster. Find what works for your dog and keep him happy!

Now we move to the great outdoors. No fences. Hopefully you have a people-food treat so enticing that your dog will leave everything else to respond to the command. If he does not come when called, let him drag a twenty- or fifty-foot light rope attached to a harness so you can retain physical control. It must be a harness outdoors. I recommend a fifty-foot light rope for a standard poodle and a ten-footer for a Chihuahua.

If these strategies are not yielding the results that you want or need, you may want to consider using an electric shock collar or e-collar. A good e-collar will enable you to use tone (sound), collar vibration, and stim (electric shock), which can be effective *if used properly*. Even if your dog is 150 yards away, the e-collar allows you to get his attention. Learning is best done with the guidance of a pro. Do not figure it out on your own, especially if you are dealing with predatory aggression. When I recommend the use of an e-collar, I am always present to instruct the owner in its proper usage. *Always.* I'm a "depends" trainer. The intensity of the need for "Leave it," depends on the sensitivity and responsiveness of the dog.

To begin, I tell dog owners to put the e-collar on the dog without activating it, read the instruction manual, and leave the remote in the box until I get there. By the time I arrive, Stubborn Scottish Terrier will have forgotten about the new collar on his neck. This is to avoid him getting "collar wise," thinking he only has to behave when the collar is on. I then do the lesson with the e-collar, making sure the dog owner understands how to use the e-collar properly.

Like the plate with meat on the floor, I tell owners to be prepared with several things planted to tempt their dog so they can practice the "Leave it" command. It can be a tennis ball rubbed with a piece of cheese, whatever. If Stubborn Scotty, wearing the activated e-collar, comes across the cheesy tennis ball and leaps two feet in the air when I call out "Leave it," there's no need for vibe or stim. If the reaction to the tone is a yawn, I go to vibe. If that too elicits a yawn, I continue on to stim. Some e-collars have a stim intensity that goes from one to one hundred. I have never, ever, used stim on a dog without stimming my own hand first. On a one to one hundred e-collar, I've often felt close to nothing at seven or ten. I need to know what the dog will be feeling and judge what is appropriate, again, depending. For a large aggressive dog with the sensitivity of a rhino, I'll use a stronger stim than I would for a Chihuahua.

You may notice that many of the e-collar instruction booklets suggest that you start with a very low stim and raise it as is necessary. I *absolutely disagree*. In my experience, doing it that way—starting low and raising the stim level because the dog adapted to the lower level—is self-defeating. The last thing I want is for the corrections to get harsher and harsher. I start at a level that shuts down the unwanted behavior immediately and enables me to consistently bring the stim level down because Stubborn Scotty becomes very sensitive to the command "Leave it." It also enables me to replace stim with tone or vibe. If the command "Leave it," is instantly followed by tone, then stim, very quickly you may find that you don't need stim at all. Stubborn Scotty will cooperate on the "Leave it" tone to avoid the stim. Soon you will only need to say "Leave it," which is the ultimate goal.

CHAPTER 7

HOW DO I REMOVE MY CHILD'S TOY FROM MY DOG WHEN HE IS GROWLING AT ME?

Resource guarding, also known as possessive aggression, can take many forms. It's one of the multiple reasons dogs present aggression, and it's not relegated to any one breed. Let's say you get a seven-week-old Lab puppy and name him Keeper because he just looks so cute whenever you give him a chew toy and he wraps his paws around it and gives little barks when you take the toy away. The resource here is the toy, and he's guarding it from being taken away. When he's twelve weeks old, you don't think anything of it when his body stiffens when you go to give him a pet while he's eating at his food bowl. When he's five months old, he's growling if you get too close when he's eating. You figure he doesn't want to be bothered so you give him space when he's eating. The resource now is the food, and he's making sure you know he has no intention of sharing. Keeper will likely be quicker to aggress over a rawhide than a ball because the ball is often shared for a game of fetch, but not necessarily. The resource guarder is also more likely to get tough with an item he knows he's not supposed to play with.

A good example of resource guarding comes from the dog of one of my clients living on the Upper East Side of Manhattan. My client held a party with chicken wings on the menu, and after a while, her vizsla made that garbage can full of chicken bones her own. She sat under the garbage can in waiting and wasn't about to share its booty with anyone. The tearful owner told me that her vizsla attacked the next person who came to dump his paper plate with the chicken bones. That party situation was a first.

Another of my more memorable possessive aggression jobs was with a Petit Basset Griffon Vendéen, the French version of a basset hound. I entered an apartment on the Upper West Side of Manhattan, and in the middle of the huge, formal living room sat the food bowl; right there in the middle of this humongous room, on a little place mat. The dog didn't drag it there, it was there on purpose. If the food bowl was placed at the far end of the kitchen, you couldn't walk by the kitchen, let alone enter without Bob seriously threatening to bite. Serving the bowl in the living room was the only place far enough away for the residents to roam the rest of the apartment without being bullied by their own dog. Do you think your dog would give up a delicious baby back rib if it slipped out of your hand onto the floor? Think he'd be real cooperative about giving up that resource? Keep in mind that the guarding can be directed toward both people and dogs. Another client of mine had to be hospitalized after trying to break up her two large dogs who were fighting over a baby back rib. I've met a few "Keepers" who'd give you a real hard time when you tried to get them to stop chewing your shoe and drop it. To a dog, it's through the nose, meaning the stronger it smells, the better. When you come home and your dog smells your pants, he knows who you touched, what you ate, and what environment you were in. That's why Mark Twain said, "If dogs could talk, nobody would own them." The stronger it smells, the better—be it shoes, hats, underpants—even dirty diapers.

It's important to know that the resource can also be a person. Grandma is sitting on the couch cuddling her toy poodle, who starts growling furiously when toddler grandson approaches Grammy. The resource is Grammy, and toy poodle ain't sharing with the kid. Possessive aggression sometimes overlaps with territorial aggression, so a dog might get aggressive with another dog over what he deems is his territory. The rear car seat location can serve as a location resource that a dog may not want to share with another dog. The bottom line is that a dog may perceive anything as a possible resource worth protecting. That's why "Leave it" and "Drop it" are important commands. Observe your dog's body language before reaching for the lollipop in your dog's mouth that your kid just dropped.

The "Drop it" command is often confused with the "Leave it" command, but they are really quite different. "Leave it" should be used before your dog gets the item in his (empty) mouth, and "Drop It" when he already got the item in his (full) mouth and has to let it go. The "it" in "Drop it," refers to anything your dog has that you want him to drop. This list includes but is certainly not limited to: discarded chicken bones, your child's toy, your reading glasses, underpants, the TV clicker, whatever. The "Leave it" command is discussed extensively in Part 8.

The "Drop it" lesson should start prior to a situation that has escalated to where your dog is growling, so that your dog will cooperate with the command. Once again, you want success to build on success, so I wouldn't suggest starting with the chicken bone, but rather something less dear to your dog like a child's toy. If your dog has the toy in his mouth, with one hand hold a treat an inch from his nose, and with your other hand under his muzzle say, "Drop it." As he drops the toy into your hand in exchange for the more valuable treat, praise him very happily with a "thank you" while giving him the treat. Do this multiple times and you will be amazed at how fast your dog gets conditioned to cooperate with the "Drop it" command.

I would be remiss in talking about the "Drop it" command if I neglected to mention working with the stubborn, growling dog that flips you the bird in lieu of cooperating. Let me set the scene: Odin picks up a chicken bone and when I tell him to "Drop it," his growl response says, "Don't even think about trying to make me unless you want to bleed!" What am I going to offer this guy to get him to trade? Honestly, nothing. I boarded and trained a 120-pound mixed breed named Zeus that would literally maim someone rather than drop anything. In every other way Zeus was a pleasure to live with and his owners adored him, but they were on the verge of having him euthanized because he was so threatening if you tried to get him to drop his acquisition. I was the owner's final effort to change his behavior. I'll tell you what I did, with the understanding that this should only be done by a pro. *In no uncertain terms, I am not recommending that you try this with your dog. Performed improperly or with the wrong kind of dog, it is very possible to collapse the trachea or otherwise severely injure your dog. In addition, you, the owner, may find also yourself injured.* Zeus loved to chew on wood, so I came up with a plan. With a leash attached to a regular metal collar and me standing directly in front of him, I dropped a small branch that he, of course, immediately grabbed. I told him to drop it. Given his history, I wasn't surprised when he growled and shook it. I responded by applying a steady pressure to the leash and pulling straight up, cutting off his air. This also prevented him from launching himself forward to bite me. His snarling and growling became so loud and fierce that my wife came to the door to see what was going on. With steady pressure upward, practically pushing my arm strength to its limit, and his front feet hardly touching the ground, Zeus finally shook his head from lack of air, opened his mouth, and dropped the branch. I immediately released the pressure and told him what a good boy he was, as I gave him a treat. A few minutes later, I dropped the branch again, but this time he dropped it after about twenty seconds of protesting. By the end of the day, he dropped the branch immediately, even though I had rubbed it with a piece of Swiss cheese, increasing the intensity of the distraction through which he cooperated. Zeus lived happily with his family to the ripe old age of thirteen.

CHAPTER 8

HOW DO I CONVINCE MY DOG TO ACCEPT MY NEW BOYFRIEND INSTEAD OF SNARLING AT HIM?

So, you broke up with your boyfriend two months ago and there seems to be a very promising "new significant other" (NSO) becoming a reality. As a matter of fact, you're already head over heels in love and it feels very mutual with NSO, but there's a problem. Now that your old boyfriend is out of the picture, your dog Rebuff has no intention of sharing you with this new interloper, and he makes his feelings crystal clear by being about as cuddly as a cactus.

In dog training (and in life) it's easier to prevent than to correct, so if you anticipate this possible problem after a breakup, here's what I suggest. Set up a first date for your NSO and your dog. Do not have your NSO come to your door. Instead, have Rebuff with you when you casually meet NSO somewhere outside, near your home. Meeting outside will eliminate most dogs' territorial response at the door when a stranger enters. Slip NSO some of Rebuff's favorite treats and take a walk together. Every so often, your NSO should ask Rebuff to sit, and then reward him with a treat and a lot of praise when he cooperates. Then, it's back to the house to drop off Rebuff and go out on your date. If NSO meets you near Rebuff's dinner time, have NSO fill the food bowl and give it to Rebuff when you get back to the house to drop him off. Perhaps ask NSO to breathe into a tissue that is placed under the food bowl. I call these "positive associations." Rebuff will be totally aware of NSO's scent as he's enjoying his meal. If the only time Rebuff gets people food is when NSO drops it in his food bowl or rewards him for sitting with a piece of chicken, how can Rebuff not love this new guy?

But what if it's already too late to create this initial positive association? You didn't anticipate this problem, and you're reading this because Rebuff is aptly named when it comes to this NSO. Well, the approach would basically be the same. Meet away from the house. Have NSO be the only person on earth who gives Rebuff people-food treats for simple cooperative responses such as sitting on command. Whenever and wherever possible, have dates that include Rebuff, such as picnics at parks, so Rebuff starts associating NSO with fun times as opposed to always taking you away. I'd also suggest that you start making Rebuff a little more independent from you. If Rebuff is accustomed to sleeping in your bed, perhaps you get him accustomed to sleeping in his own. You're old enough to decide who you want to share with! You can be sure that Rebuff is cognizant of the importance of your bed. He perceives the apartment as the den. That's why he's territorial at the door and doesn't pee or poop indoors. Dogs keep their den clean. He recognizes the bed as your inner den, where you spend many hours in repose; it's a significant place to a dog. Get Rebuff out before you want to share it with a two-legged significant other instead of your four-legged one. (By the way, if the NSO isn't willing to help with the relationship, I suggest you rebuff him.)

I've seen it quite a few times when a boyfriend or girlfriend moves in, and to the chagrin of the dog, the pack of two becomes a pack of three. Rebuff may have been fine with sharing his two-legged significant other (TLSO) when the boyfriend came over for short-stay visits. But for Rebuff to have to share his TLSO, and his den, and his time on a *permanent* basis is *unacceptable*.

Here are a couple of tips to help thaw the ice and go a long way to helping your dog see the household as a pack of three instead of two plus an interloper.

Tip 1: Just like in the other scenarios, have NSO feed your dog his meals.

Tip 2: Put a harness on your dog and let him drag a leash around in the home. When NSO is going to move about the house, have him pick up the leash and take your dog with him. Tell NSO to offer him treats as they're moving about.

Tip 3: When the three of you are hanging out, have NSO call your dog to come from time to time, and when the dog arrives, give him a treat. All these treats are the size of crumbs. It's not the size that counts, it's the association.

Tip 4: If your dog is truly underfoot, another strategy to consider is using the "Leave it" command. This command is usually used to instruct a dog to leave another dog, a squirrel, rabbit, deer, slipper, ice cream that wound up on the sidewalk—and your NSO. Whatever you want him to leave. I discuss the "Leave it" command in depth in Part 8.

CHAPTER 9

WHAT SHOULD I DO IF MY DOG GETS INTO A FIGHT?

Mark Twain said, "If you love what you do, you'll never work a day in your life." And that describes me. I like to say I made my living getting paid to play intelligently with dogs. Best job in the world! Yet, in spite of what Twain said, even the best job will have its difficult days and will be work-work, not fun-work.

My lessons generally fall into one of two groups: manners and problems. Of my average fifteen to twenty training appointments per week, half were for basic manners, like not peeing on the expensive white shag carpet or crotch-sniffing your pastor when he or she comes to visit, helping oneself to the turkey on Thanksgiving while the whole family is in the den toasting their good fortune, or sending Dad to the chiropractor after every "tug of war" walk. The other half should have been more fun because they were more challenging. The worst behavioral problem is aggression toward people. However, dog-on-dog aggression is next on the list. Too often, these lessons initially had me dealing with such vicious aggression that it was very serious work-work, definitely not fun-work. The way I deal with dog-on-dog aggression depends on the intensity of the aggression. For example, a dog biting another dog and "completely losing it" tells me that the intensity level is very strong.

All dogs contain aggression within, but each dog's individual level of inner-aggression comes down to a matter of thresholds and intensity. Push the right button and see how quickly the dog aggresses. What's his threshold? And just as important, what's the intensity and duration of the presented aggression? I've seen a few cases where a friendly dog that was mauled by another dog became a consummate dog fighter—"the best defense is a good offense," as they say. I had a client in NYC with a Rotty that hated and lunged at all standard poodles because a neighbor's standard poodle growled and lunged at him when he was a puppy. Talk about discriminatory profiling! I remember a client in NYC whose beagle got so crazed at the sight of another dog that I wouldn't have been able to get the dog's attention if I hit him over the head with a baseball bat. Let's look at this from two angles, preventing a fight from occurring in the first place and what to do once a fight is already in progress.

Preventing a Fight

If your dog seems hell-bent on attacking a dog or has already attacked a dog and another altercation seems inevitable, like the beagle that I worked with who would go absolutely berserk when he saw another dog, your dog needs to be taught "Leave it," "Look at me," and "Heel." While I'm talking here about the "Leave it" command to address dog-on-dog aggression, it is in fact an effective tool for a variety of situations. I don't believe a dog is properly trained if he doesn't comply with this command. Your dog should walk away from any object, animal, or person, no matter how enticing, when he hears you say "Leave it!" I talk extensively about the "Leave it" command in Part 8.

I begin by applying the "Leave It" command to everything except dogs because I don't want the dog to relate the command exclusively to dogs. I want the dog to understand that he should "leave" anything that he's focused on when I say "Leave it!" So, with Beagle, I started by putting a vibration collar on him and having someone put a plate with a hamburger on it on the floor. When Beagle was about to grab the burger, I told him to "Leave it," and pushed the button on the remote, which caused the collar on his neck to vibrate, startling him into stopping in his tracks. Then, he got treats and praise for leaving it. This lesson was repeated with many different foods and objects. When his indoor "Leave it" was consistent and reliable, we moved outside where he was tempted by squirrels. With success building on success, we finally reached dogs.

The "Look at me" command is a form of redirection. You're hanging out watching TV and, as Scrappy walks by, you say "Look at me" with a little intensity. Unlike a cat, your dog's natural instinct will be to look at you. The moment he makes eye contact, you give him a treat with a lot of praise. Do that twenty to thirty times and Scrappy will be walking up to you, looking you in the face, nose to nose, trying to manipulate you into giving him a treat. He only gets light praise. Scrappy has to hear "Look at me" to garner the treat and heavy praise. Once that's working beautifully, introduce the distractions. When you can throw a treat across the room or put the food bowl down and he responds to your "Look at me" instead of dashing after the edibles, he's ready for the great outdoors. I cannot overstate the importance of success building on success. When the offending dog is across the street or half a block away, start Scrappy looking at you instead of the dog that he thinks he needs to show who's boss. *Success!* Continue with your favorable outcomes until you can walk past another dog and Scrappy's ignoring the interloper, looking at you for his reward.

In my experience, you and your dog will probably need the help of a pro to teach your dog to heel successfully. The "Heel" command can be considered a form of redirection. When your dog is heeling, he is by your left knee and he never strays from there. *That's all he's doing.* He's not sniffing stuff, he's not peeing, he's not "doin' nothing" but staying by your left knee. Whether you're walking slowly, making continuous left turns, about faces, running, sudden stops, whatever, he's at your left knee. Let me break it down for you.

Standing still, with Scrappy on my left side at my knee, I say "Heel" and start walking, taking the first step with my left foot. He will quickly get conditioned that when my left foot moves, he moves. And it's always the left foot first. If I were to move with the right foot first, it would confuse Scrappy's understanding of "Heel." Loose leash is critical when teaching "Heel." When I give the command "Heel" and start walking, Scrappy's typical reaction will be to immediately forge ahead. I do not hold him back, keeping the leash loose. This is where timing is important. I make a sharp U-turn when Scrappy is close to the end of the six-foot leash. When he hits the end of the leash, Scrappy will be startled by the taut and uncomfortable leash and wonder "What happened? Where is Tom?" My response is to walk in the opposite direction whenever Scrappy is not paying attention and staying by my left knee. If Scrappy starts veering left, I make a sharp right. If he starts cutting me off, heading right, I make a sharp left into his face. If he walks slowly, I break into a run. The timing has to be perfect because I want Scrappy's attitude to become "Holy Moly! I've got to pay attention to this idiot that is always going the wrong way 'cuz when we're not together, it's real uncomfortable." Scrappy will get tired of being startled by hitting the end of the leash because I'm going in another direction. He will start staying at my left knee and paying close attention so he can't be caught off guard at the end of the leash. When Scrappy is heeling well, I praise him quietly and, periodically, offer treats. Even off leash, my dog Paula Jean will ignore everything to stay next to me when I say heel.

Breaking Up a Fight

Most humans, when they see a neighbor or person they don't like, don't attack. They simply ignore that person. Often with dogs, this is not the case. They attack! The same dog who usually shows you love and respect will likely bite you severely when you try to break up the fight. This is called redirected or displacement aggression. Do not jump in and try to break up the fight! Lots of dogs being trained for police work "wash out" because of displacement aggression presented during training. They bite the handler in frustration if they can't get the "acting bad guy." When sufficiently aroused (not sexually) a displacement biter may bite the nearest person or object.

Here's the easier scenario. You're out with your dog for a walk when you meet someone also out with his dog. Both pugilists are on leash. They go through the proverbial sniffing as the owners neglect to perceive their dogs' body language displaying discomfort. The violence erupts and you both pull them apart with the leashes. Engaged in an actual fight, verbal commands are useless.

Now the harder scenario: both pugilists are off leash. When the violence erupts, don't bend down to reach in and grab them. Remember, one of the multiple types of aggression is displacement aggression. In a serious fight with another dog, both dogs will bite whatever they can reach, especially anything touching them. My Doberman Michelle, who was a working search dog, had a best friend, a large white shepherd named Daisy. They spent many years playing and hiking together. One time though their roughhousing got carried away and they got into a fight. I kicked them apart and hurt the top of my foot on the bony part of one of their muzzles. I was lucky not to get bitten. I recently saw a young lady who was hospitalized from the bite wounds she incurred in her house while breaking up her two large brawling dogs. I taught the dogs several routines to decrease possible arousal and arguments over food, treats, people coming and going, attention, etc. In case of a possible recurrence, they're now both dragging four-foot leashes and there's an air horn strategically located with the hope that a blast on that will momentarily stun them into separating. The owner also has a big whisk broom strategically placed to slap them apart if necessary.

Bottom line, there's no easy answer to breaking up a serious quarrel. Best suggestions? First, your dog needs to socialize with lots of dogs so he expects friendly play with the dogs he meets rather than being nervous around them. Second, the dog owner should have some awareness of his dog's body language in order to recognize when he communicates discomfort as well as reading the possible discomfort of the other dog in the encounter. If discomfort is detected, it's a good to time to give your dog the "Heel" command and pass the other dog without a meeting. If your dog isn't completely cooperative or is still showing interest in the other dog, throw in a "Leave it."

CHAPTER 10

WHY IS MY DOG MORE AGGRESSIVE ON LEASH THAN OFF LEASH?

Meet my versions of Dr. Jekyll and Mr. Hyde. It all started when I went to the dog park with Dr. Jekyll and his owner. Dr. Jekyll was your basic golden retriever, weighing about seventy pounds and as smart as one expects a golden to be. Upon entering the seventy-five acre no-fence dog park, I took his leash off. We decided to walk the trails that circled the open fields and met another golden retriever within five minutes. After the proverbial "getting to know each other via nose," we all spent the next half hour hanging out together while hiking the trails. There was no sign of any kind of anxiety or ill-will whatsoever.

The following day, Dr. Jekyll along with his owner and I, took a walk down Main Street in Vineyard Haven with Dr. Jekyll on leash. We turned the corner and I noticed the dog with whom he had amiably hiked the day before. The moment Dr. Jekyll saw the other dog, I observed his metamorphosis from Dr. Jekyll to Mr. Hyde. I truly expected that when we got close enough for Mr. Hyde to recognize yesterday's friend, he would change back to Dr. Jekyll, but no such luck. He stayed Mr. Hyde, going up on his rear legs and clearly displaying an aggression suggesting he wished to vanquish yesterday's friend.

Even a well socialized dog is much more likely to be aggressive on a leash than off. You may think that your dog is protecting you, but actually, your dog feels as though *you're* protecting *him*. He might be much bolder with his physical connection to you. That leash connection says to him: "I got your back." It's like a little kid feeling pretty tough with his big brother standing behind him. Dogs are creatures of habit and Dr. Jekyll/Mr. Hyde had become accustomed to being aggressive on leash. Even though he had enjoyed this other dog's company the day before, he was now taking on the role of a tough guy with his big brother having his back. Solution: train him to be a well-socialized dog. A good place to start is teaching your dog that when he sees another dog on a leash, his attitude should be, *This could become my BFF*. I talk about this in detail in Chapter 18.

CHAPTER 11

WHAT ARE SOME OF THE LIMITS OF ROUGHHOUSING WITH MY DOG?

Roughhousing. To do? Or not to do? That is the question. Humans do it all the time! Wrestling on the floor with friends is probably a part of most boys' childhood. I'm post-childhood and still roughhousing, but now it's with my kids and grandkids. However, we don't have razor-sharp teeth! And that's the difference between us two-leggeds and our four-legged charges. Teeth.

Dogs love to roughhouse, but their hands are their teeth. Roughhousing is play fighting, and more often than not includes a lot of growling, mouthing, and playful biting known as bite restriction. Bite restriction is reinforced when a puppy accidentally bites another pup too hard, causing a yelp of pain or an angry response, teaching the biter to be gentler. Most puppies come from the litter with a decent modicum of bite restriction. Breeders with a one-dog litter will often look to have their puppy spend time with a similarly aged multiple-dog litter just to learn puppy play and bite restriction.

In spite of the fact that it's normal for dogs, I've always taught that teeth and our flesh are a "no no." I often see clients letting their brand-new puppy nibble on their fingers. My immediate response to the new dog owner is, "You're not a chew toy! Teeth and flesh are the last thing you want Ruffy to get accustomed to. Substitute! Shove a toy in pup's mouth." As a puppy, young punk, or adult, your dog will be using mouth and teeth with any kind of sustained wrestling, so have a tug of war instead, but with rules. Even when the eight-week-old puppy is trying to play tough guy with your hand, avoid having teeth and flesh meet. Teach Ruffy to cooperate when you say "Drop it." In lieu of play fighting, teach tricks, retrieving with name recognition, go find, whatever.

DOG TRAINING DIARY

THE GOLDEN HEART AND THE
DOG SHE RESCUED

"A parakeet is nice, like a feather on a hat,
but a dog is a mensch."
—Enid Shomer

"Get control immediately, get rid of the dog, or leave" is
what the co-op board told a tearful Eunice before she
called me. "The dog" was Daniel, an approximately
four-year-old mutt that weighed eighty pounds and was half-black-
half-white in splotches. I saw touches of shepherd, hound, and
Dalmatian in Daniel. He had hanging hound ears, dark menacing
eyes, and a wiry black tail that usually rested at three-quarters up—
except when he aggressed—then it shot straight up for a second
before whipping straight out like a saber, horizontal to his body,
as he flew into full attack mode. Having been his target, I was
unfortunate enough to observe this tail communication firsthand.
Daniel wasn't much into giving warning signals. He just fired.

Eunice was one of the good guys: she had taken Daniel off
death row and rescued him from the pound about a month before.

Daniel wasn't the first, but he was definitely the worst. Eunice is a shelter dog foster parent, but Daniel was a keeper because, as Eunice said when she called me, "How do I place him?" I pointed out that keeping him may end her ability to foster more dogs if Daniel wants to eat them.

"Well, that's also one of the reasons why I called you, to teach Daniel to accept other dogs."

"Dogs?" I said. "What about people? I thought you said he was people-aggressive, seriously people-aggressive."

"Well, yes," she sighed. "That's first. When can you come and how do you want to meet?"

When she asked "How do you want to meet?" I assumed immediately that coming to her door to pick her and Daniel up was out of the question.

One of the aggressions is territoriality. This is why dogs bark at the door, and it's why I don't meet the Daniels of the world at the threshold of their own domain. "Eunice," I said. "Before we pick a time and place, tell me more about Daniel."

She referred to Daniel as a terror. Most of the times when dog owners describe their dog as a "terror," it's used in a comedic sense: the dog gets into everything, causes never-ending mischief—a real terror.

This wasn't the case here. Daniel was the real deal. After listening for a few minutes, I said, "So let me get this straight, Eunice. Your vet told you to seriously consider euthanizing him. You've been unable to have any company since you got him, not a friend or family member, and forget about a boyfriend. You even fear for the pizza delivery guys and you worry and fret all day about the next walk. Not to mention you're trying to change your life's routines to accommodate a ridiculous walking schedule."

"I don't think it's ridiculous," she said defensively.

So often I need to point out to clients the insane lengths to which they go in adapting to their dog's behavior. "Eunice," I retorted. "You just said you really hope the weather is terrible whenever you walk him because you're least likely to meet other humans or dogs. Like in the middle of the night and during hurricanes! On top of that, you think you're becoming a clinical nervous wreck, which is understandable when you're confronted by the realization several times a day that you have to put a leash on Daniel and head out into the real world."

I then took a moment to catch my breath and let what I had said sink in. "Eunice," I continued. "It's time to take your life back. If you spoke to a shrink, he'd tell you the same thing: your life is in crisis primarily because of the dog; fix your relationship with the dog or get rid of it. The question is 'How do I fix it?' That's why you called me, which is a concrete step toward getting your life back. What's going on now is not a good way to live," I said. "It's time for a change."

"Well, if you put it that way it does sound crazy, the way I'm living right now," she conceded. "But, I'm not putting him down! I don't care what my vet says," she finished vehemently.

"Eunice, I would never suggest that a dog be put down without my ever having met that dog," I said, treading cautiously. "But, there's one thing I want to make sure of. You said that Daniel never showed you any aggression whatsoever."

"No . . ." she said.

"So," I continued, "if you dropped a sparerib on the floor and Danny Boy got it and you were afraid he'd choke on it, could you take it from him?"

Without hesitation she said, "Yes." It was hard to believe, but she sounded believable.

Two days later I was parked across the street from her first-floor co-op unit and observed her leaving with Daniel. I was delighted to see that Daniel was really acclimated to his Gentle Leader, just as Eunice had said. I love the Gentle Leader. It's a face collar using the same principle that empowers a 150-pound person to maneuver a 1,000-pound horse. If I pull you by your nose, your head and body will immediately follow with little resistance. I've probably acclimated hundreds of dogs to the Gentle Leader, and with every single one I asked the owner, "If I pull you by your nose, what's going to follow?" Out of the thousand or so times I've posed that question, the answer was almost always "The rest of me," or something like it. The two exceptions were basically identical: "My fist in your face" and "A punch in the nose." I chose to tread carefully with those two. The Gentle Leader is effective and humane and enables a 100-pound person to walk a 100-pound dog without going airborne if the dog pulls.

Daniel's six-foot leather leash was also attached to a metal prong collar. The Gentle Leader controls with leverage while the prong collar controls with pain. At the other end of the leash was Eunice. Her large brown eyes were anxious as she looked around for anything that might incite mayhem and trauma with her dog. Her car was a small white four-door SUV. Instead of opening a rear door and allowing Daniel to enter when she said "Okay," Eunice opened the driver's door, at which point Daniel (who was standing next to her) bumped her aside while jumping into the driver's seat—and then stayed there. I couldn't believe what came next.

Eunice, using her whole body, literally, physically, was trying to shove Daniel into the next seat. At first, I was terrified by the imminent possibility of a face bite, but as time went on, it got funnier and funnier. It would have been great on *America's Funniest Home Videos*. Eunice was yelling at Daniel to move over, kind of a playful yelling while trying to shove her way into the seat with Daniel passive-aggressively being deadweight leaning into her.

This was a classic case of dominant aggression or resource guarding or both. The resource here was the seat itself. It's the location where "driver" sits, best seat in the house. This scenario, shoving an aggressive dog out of the coveted seat using head and shoulders, can easily result in a lightning-fast bite and tragedy, unless you have "that type" of relationship with the dog. And evidently Eunice did. This was their routine; it was a game they played. Daniel was having fun playing deadweight and they were both enjoying the playful shoving and banter, with Eunice saying happily, "Move over, stupid-head," while shoving Daniel over.

Not the slightest indication of aggression from Daniel did I see, and after my heart stopped pounding from fear, it was beautiful. She had a great relationship with her dog. Eunice persisted and eventually Daniel moved over.

Where to go and what to do was already prearranged. Eight minutes later we were about fifteen car widths apart in a pretty large mall parking lot. It wasn't too crowded. Casually leaning against my back fender, I watched Eunice and Daniel both trying to exit the car, like Archie Bunker and Mike Stivic trying to get through the doorway. It was a tie as they hit the asphalt.

As they approached I was thankful that Daniel wasn't pulling on the lead. The best way to approach a dog like this is to not approach him at all. The owner and dog control the approach so that the nervous or aggressive dog isn't put in the position of having no control whatsoever as a dog or person is coming at him. So, Eunice and I pretended to be meeting each other by accident. We greeted each other and then had a low-key casual conversation, all the while I was completely ignoring Daniel. I made no eye contact and didn't relate to him in any way. "Bore the Dog" was the name of the game. When I deemed Daniel sufficiently bored, we started walking with Daniel on Eunice's left and me on her right. Head and tail erect, wary eye on anyone potentially invading our space, Daniel was clearly on guard, not sauntering along, not relaxed.

"What do you want me to do?" Eunice said in a shaky voice.

"Well, for one thing," I replied, "I want you to take a few deep, relaxing breaths and appreciate the fact that we're walking together like this with no problem. Also, Eunice, please stop saying his name every few seconds whenever he shows any interest in sniffing something. I understand you're trying to hold his interest, but what you're really doing is teaching him to ignore his name and ignore you. Could you imagine just the two of us taking a half-hour walk and I said 'Eunice, Eunice' every few seconds? You'd not only never walk with me again, you'd also probably change your name."

She laughed at that, causing Daniel to notice, and that was good because "laugh" equals "relax."

"One other thing," I continued. "Leash handling is critical, and one of the most critical parts of leash handling is having the right amount of leash between you and your dog. The goal is to always have a loose leash, a leash with slack in it. You translate tension to a dog through a tight leash, but it has to be the right amount of slack. Too much slack and your timing on everything is off; too little and he's pulling, or it's you physically restricting him instead of him cooperating. It needs to be loose, but a split second away from being tight, if need be."

The more we walked, the more relaxed Eunice became. "This is great!" she exclaimed. "I can't believe he's this relaxed with you here, that he's letting you come along."

"I didn't come along to you," I said. "Remember, you two came to me. Also, he's not that relaxed, but he is tolerating me."

We were ready for the next step. "Now, Eunice," I said. "I want you to do me a favor and disconnect the leash from the prong collar. It looks like it needs a couple of extra links because it's engaging about the same time as the Gentle Leader and I don't want him to feel pain every time the leash gets tight. The prong collar should be a backup in case he slips the Gentle Leader—which by the way, if he does get it off his nose, he's not loose. It just slips down to his neck and serves as a collar."

"Disconnect the collar?" she said incredulously. "Are you sure?"

"Absolutely," I said with calm conviction. "And Eunice, talk to him as you disconnect from the prong collar. Keep him relaxed with your praise. Tell him 'Good boy' with some gentle petting. As the behavior is happening you let the dog know that either you like it or you don't. That's training. Timing is key."

Daniel was unperturbed.

After about ten minutes of strolling and making small talk I said, "In a few minutes I'm going to ask you to hand me the leash." She stopped abruptly and stared at me, kind of frozen. "Keep walking!" I urged. "Relax, Eune." She had told me her friends called her Eune and she liked the nickname. "Relax and smile. Smile because of how much your life is going to improve because of this."

She looked really worried and said, "Why don't we call it a day and talk about your holding the leash for the next lesson."

"Eune, I'm not the behaviorist who had you fill out a ten-page questionnaire and then prescribed drugs. I'm very hands-on. I'm always hands-on! As the song goes, 'Take it to the limit, one more time.' That's what a trainer should do, with success building on success: take it as far as he can, to the limit. I want as much successful interaction with Daniel as possible."

And so we walked and talked for another fifteen minutes or so and then I had Eunice surreptitiously hand me the leash as she casually slowed down and stepped around Daniel's back so that he was now walking between us with me holding the leash. At this point the big question becomes, "What happens when the dog realizes that a stranger is holding the leash?"

Usually nothing happens. Territorial aggression is basically eliminated when the known territory disappears. Aggressive territorial responses are most vigorous when a dog is behind a fence, roped to a tree, in a car, behind a window or door, or on a leash held by the owner. In most of these cases the dogs appear very strong and protective, but in reality, these dogs are buoyed by the protection of the fence, the surrounding car, the window, the door, and especially by the owner at the other end of the leash. Walk the dog into a gas station, he loves the gas station attendant, but put him in the car, he's bouncing off the car windows wanting to kill the same gas station attendant. Plenty of dogs are like that.

So, if Daniel displayed any aggression now it would probably be dominant or fear aggression, but as we continued walking I kept some slack in the leash and gave him some room to slow down and sniff something. We walked out of the parking lot and crossed the street to walk around the block. This gave me the opportunity to ask a lot of questions, not to mention that the expression "a tired dog is a well-behaved dog" is extremely valid. I gathered that Daniel hardly got any exercise based on the fact that Eunice was so fearful of walking him.

It took about two seconds for Daniel to realize that I had the leash, at which point he stopped walking, causing Eunice to hesitate. "Keep moving, keep up with me!" I urged Eunice as I slowly kept moving forward, letting the six-foot leash slide slowly through my hands so as not to pull on him at this point. Eunice caught up with me just as I ran out of leash and would be forced to either stop or pull him forward. Daniel tolerated the light tug from me because he wanted to catch up with Mom.

We kept walking and talking. "You know, Eunice," I said. "You guys are doing great. For a while there, Daniel was more relaxed than you, but then, that's not saying much. Now he's pretty relaxed and actually beginning to find the walk interesting."

With a twinkle in her eye, Eunice replied, "I'm beginning to slow down my hyperventilating, thank you very much."

"He's a handsome guy. Do you brush him?" I asked.

"When he lets me."

"Do you use treats?"

"Yes, after I'm done he gets a nice treat."

"Eunice," I said. "Remember my saying: 'Training a dog is letting the dog know you like the behavior or not, *as the behavior is happening.*' Let him chew on treats *while* you're brushing him. When we get back to the cars I want you to write a bunch of things down so you don't forget them."

"What, now I have to take notes?" she complained.

"With me, everyone takes notes! Now, where does he sleep?" I continued.

"With me, in bed, but before you start telling me how bad that is, let me just say—"

I interrupted her here: "Eunice, Eunice, you don't need to defend yourself, you're one of the good guys. You're trying to save a life here! You think you're the only person who sleeps with their dog? I'm not judging you, but I will make suggestions based on my knowledge of K-9 behavior. Here are some more questions: Where does he sleep? On your pillow or at the foot of the bed?"

"Wherever he wants, though usually at the foot."

"Has he ever growled at you while on the bed?"

I loved her honesty. She didn't hesitate: "A few times," she replied. "When I shove him with my foot to get him out of my space he growls. I just keep shoving and tell him to shut up."

"And that's that?" I was somewhat incredulous. "No escalation of growling or snap?" Then I remembered the "shoving out of the driver's seat" show she and Daniel had just put on.

"No, he buys it," she told me. "He just kind of sighs with annoyed resignation." I believed her. But when I asked if she could get him out of the bed if she wanted to, she hesitated. "I don't know," she said. "Maybe."

"So Eune, you're not sure if you could get Daniel out of your bed if you wanted to. Let me put it to you this way: don't you think you're old enough to decide who you want to share your bed with? Maybe you should start calling him Mr. Daniel," I teased.

She laughed heartily at that, and the more she laughed, the more relaxed Mr. Daniel appeared to be.

"Ready for the next step?" I said jauntily.

"What's that?" she said suspiciously.

"I'm going to slowly stop walking with Mr. D. but you're going to keep walking away at the same pace, not looking back. When you get to that bench by the blue car near the end of the block, have a seat."

Obviously anxious, she said, "What are you going to do then?"

"I don't know. It depends." I tell people I'm an "it depends" trainer. What I do depends on what the dog does.

"Keep walking to the bench, Eunice, keep walking!" I had to say it a couple of times as I slowed down to a standstill. Daniel strained against the leash to follow Mom, but the leash didn't give. The Gentle Leader turned his head toward me; I smiled and started walking at a 90-degree angle away from Eunice while saying "Let's go" with a firm tug that suggested "I expect you to cooperate." He half bucked like a horse for a split second and then came along, reluctantly.

We walked for a while, with me always choosing a direction other than where he wanted to go. When he wanted to go left I chose to go right, coaxing him along with gentle pulls and lots of praise, not to mention the prearranged treats in the form of hot dog pieces. He readily took the treats—a good sign, because if a dog is really frightened or upset it won't take any food, no matter what you offer. It's my litmus test when a dog hides behind the owner. If he takes the treat, he's not as frightened as he purports to be and he's often being quite intelligently manipulative.

I took him back to where Eunice was sitting on the bench to reassure him all was okay, had Eunice say "Hi" and give him a pet, and then walked him away again. At times, with open mouth and slight pant and softer eyes, he seemed to be getting more and more relaxed, and the more he relaxed, the more I relaxed. What the hell: by age four practically every dog has spent plenty of time walking on a leash, and Mr. D. was no exception. This wasn't new to him.

Everything was going great so far, but we hadn't encountered any dogs or people coming close, which was supposedly when he presented unbridled aggression, especially at night. This isn't unusual. Every dog I've encountered is on higher alert in the dark. My guess is that even though they have considerably better night vision than people, like us they still can't see as much as when it's light out. Almost all of us are a little less comfortable walking at night, aren't we?

But with dogs I think it's more intense because of their keen sense of smell. At night there may be far fewer people and activity about, fewer cars, less distracting white noise, fewer distracting human-caused smells, but primal smells abound. Think of all the nocturnal animals moving about, hunting and scavenging. Suburbia has its share of raccoons, rabbits, squirrels, skunks, opossums, snakes, and deer, and to a dog's nose and ears their presence is much stronger in the dark.

At this point I could have told Eunice that this was great and it was time to head back home. We had walked about with no sign of aggression and even had a stranger holding the leash. Let's leave it successful, success builds on success. But that would have been bullshit. Eunice might have said, "But you haven't seen his bad behavior or his reaction to another dog!" And she would have been totally right. I can't fix a problem if I don't see it. I need to see it. Confronting problems is part of my dog training mantra.

So, I once again went back to the bench and picked up Eunice and we continued walking, heading back to the mall parking lot. Throughout all of this I had not stopped observing Daniel closely, and his comfort level seemed to have plateaued a while ago. Half the time he wasn't happy, and therefore I didn't want to share a small sidewalk with a stranger. Hence the parking lot, where I could better control the distance between Daniel and me and any strangers we might encounter. I also decided to make him happier by letting him earn some hot dog pieces.

Within a couple of minutes, he was sitting on command and tolerating a soft pat on the head. I then took it to the next step by telling him to sit. Then, directly facing him, I held my hand out like a cop stopping traffic and said, "Wait," while making strong eye contact with him. After about ten seconds I softened my face and sang a very happy "Okay" while bending slightly and backing up a little. It brought the immediate response I wanted as Daniel trotted happily forward to receive his treat.

Turning to Eunice I explained, "Okay is a release. It doesn't mean come. If he had come to you it would have been okay. He came to me because I have the treat."

"What if he didn't stay?" was her reply.

"Right question," I answered. "I don't use the word 'no.' By the time I meet them, most dogs think their name is 'No.' I once saw a great T-shirt that had a picture of a dog meeting another dog saying, 'Hi, my name's No Bad Dog, what's yours?'"

Eunice laughed and said, "Well, if you don't say no, what do you say?"

"I just say 'Uh-uh' with a frown on my face while moving toward the dog. The intensity of my forward movement and my uh-uh depends on circumstances and the dog's reaction."

Up to this point the lesson was going great. Daniel was in Dr. Jekyll mode with no sign of Mr. Hyde, and Eunice was quite impressed. "By the way," I continued, "the reason I'm teaching him to stay is because I want him to use some self-control." At that moment Daniel was a few feet away staring casually at some people who were laughing while getting into their car.

"Danny Boy," I said, getting his attention, but as he turned toward my voice I detected a very subtle change in his demeanor. I don't know if it was his body language, the look in his eyes, or just a vibe he was giving off, but I detected a less happy dog. I thought, *Shit, I think Mr. Hyde just arrived on the scene*, so I took a non-threatening, casual half step toward him and said evenly, "Sit."

I intended to make him "wait" longer this time but changed my mind the instant I saw him "harden"—his body went rigid and his stare hard. I wouldn't defer to him, but I wasn't going to push him either, so the moment he sat I was planning to praise and treat and continue walking.

He didn't sit. I made myself bigger with a breath, faced him squarely, and moved very slightly forward with a stern face. It was then that I saw that crazy tail response. It was a snap, like a whip being snapped but staying rigid at the end of the snap.

In the next instant my whole world changed. There were two of me: my mind's eye observing me from afar in a slow-motion dance in a parking lot with a dog, and me, in the opposite of slow motion, adrenaline dumping into my circulatory system as Daniel kept coming and coming and coming. He wasn't just trying to bite me, he wanted to punish me.

The first attack was Pearl Harbor, no warning growl, no showing of teeth, just a tail snap and flying leap at my face with barred fangs. My left hand slid down the leash, eliminating the slack he was creating by coming toward me, and jerked hard to the left while sidestepping to the right. The extreme physical strength and viciousness of Daniel's attacks made me feel like I was fighting for my life. The possibility of the Gentle Leader breaking or coming

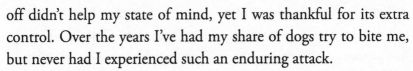
off didn't help my state of mind, yet I was thankful for its extra control. Over the years I've had my share of dogs try to bite me, but never had I experienced such an enduring attack.

My heart sounded like a parade drum pounding in my ears as the assault continued as I tried to protect myself and get Daniel to cease hostilities. It felt like I was in the Twilight Zone as the unholy dance continued like a bad dream; a snarling mouth with bared teeth repeatedly flying at my face with me jerking him to one side, sidestepping to the other side while firmly saying "Uh-uh." I was vaguely aware of people scrambling, a crowd forming, someone yelling, "Call the police!" and the sound of someone screaming: Eunice. I've always been a believer in "If it ain't working, dump it!" And what I was doing was jerking him more harshly every time he attacked, which was clearly inflaming and increasing his aggression. Continuing down this path was sure to result in injury to one or both of us.

I had all the leverage because I jerked him to the side when he was airborne, but I did it with restraint because I didn't want him to land off his feet and get injured, not to mention the more violent it got the more likely the Gentle Leader would dislodge, with me or someone else getting hurt. Not only was the situation deteriorating, but besides the extreme fear and embarrassment, I was rapidly becoming mentally and physically exhausted.

I switched to nonviolent resistance, using the leash to redirect him away from my sidestep with a pull instead of a jerk. I think it was fatigue that finally won in the end. He just stopped! And there we stood, facing each other and panting. What I did at that point I did with no forethought whatsoever, and it impressed the hell out of Eunice as well as some onlookers. I casually and non-threateningly stepped toward Daniel (of course eliminating the excess leash slack) and told him to sit. He did. I told him, "Good boy," and started heading to the car with him in tow.

"It's time to take this bad boy home," I said over my shoulder to Eunice, who was standing there in a state of shock. The car was probably 300 feet away and getting through the crowd with Daniel felt more like a journey than a 300-foot walk to a car. People were yelling out comments, all negative by the sound of the general din. It was like bad white noise, but I heard none of it. I was 110 percent focused on Daniel.

He was real tense as we passed the onlookers and their comments, fear aggression brimming just under the surface. Head down, semi-slink walk, wrinkling lip—I worried that if one of the talking heads got too close Danny Boy would fire. I acted as relaxed as I could and was able to keep tension out of the leash while saying in a very even, positive voice, "You're doing great, Daniel, good boy."

When we got to the car I asked Eunice to open the back door on the passenger side, and I ushered Daniel in, which he was happy to do. "Are you okay to drive?" I asked Eunice. She nodded. "Meet you at the house," I said as I turned and headed to my car. We needed to get out of there ASAP as a couple of the talking heads were still persisting with their harassment and threatening to call the cops.

Back at the condo we repeated the leash transfer, a short walk together with her handing me the leash, then we walked around a quiet block. I wanted to further relax and tire Daniel before going indoors. We entered Eunice's condo unit with me holding the leash and crossing the threshold first, then Eunice and Daniel. One learns best by experience (as long as the experience doesn't kill you). As a rookie, I once had an aggressive dog I'd been walking for half an hour whip around at the door to the house, right at the threshold, and try to eat me for trying to enter his domain. That was the last time a dog entered anything before or in front of me.

Once inside I chose to stand near one of his beds, leaning against a wall holding the leash, loosely, but not too loosely. "Do we have some time to talk?" I said.

"All afternoon and night," she said breathlessly. She was practically in tears. "That was fucked up!" she cried.

"Yeah," I said. "That was horrible, but I'm glad it happened. No, not glad it happened at all, but glad I saw it. Now I know what I'm really dealing with and I'm not going to underestimate him. And it ended in the parking lot with his sitting for me and walking calmly to the car, and here we are in the house, together. When was the last time you, Daniel, and a guest were sharing this living room?"

She nodded and said, "Point taken. I'll put on a fresh pot of coffee."

"Thanks, I could use it," I said, feeling totally exhausted and wishing I could sit down, which wasn't feasible with Daniel on the other end of the leash.

When she came back with the coffee, I became aware of how vulnerable I was, holding the leash with only one hand, so I put the coffee on the mantelpiece after two quick sips. "He's dangerous, Eunice," I said.

"If all you're going to tell me is to put him down, you can leave right now" was her response.

"Eunice, this is a tragedy waiting to happen. I'll help you pick out another dog and train it for free. This is my personal policy whenever someone has to go through the trauma and despair of losing a dog prematurely."

With tears in her eyes, she said, "Listen, Tom, I grew up in six different foster homes, and if there's one thing I swore to myself from my loveless, shitty upbringing, it's that I'll never quit like all the people who quit on me. Daniel loves me, has never threatened me, and I'm not going to quit and kill him, so are you going to help me, or are you going to quit?"

So, after three phone calls postponing the rest of that day's lessons, over the next two hours and two more cups of coffee, I covered as many dos and don'ts, as many "conditions" as I could think of in order for me to continue helping. I suggested a low-protein diet, Prozac, dragging a piece of leash on a Gentle Leader in the house, making him do something to earn any treats, privileges, love, and praise, how to keep him off all furniture, especially the bed, and most important, how to acclimatize him to a basket muzzle for outdoors and when she had company.

"What if I want him on furniture and my bed?" was her initial response.

"Fine," I said, "but not for a month, and then only on invitation. If he has to be on the couch with you, I repeat, not for a month, then put a towel or something on the couch and he has to stay on that when you put it on the couch, and only when you invite him up. If he gets on any furniture without your explicit invitation, you are to grab the leash, at least two feet from his neck, tell him 'Off' and gently and firmly pull him off. Never grab his collar to pull him off. Your hands are to go to him for love and praise and treats, never anything negative. Use the leash instead. If he will not let you put the muzzle on him for visitors and going outside, if he threatens you or bites you, he's done!"

Eunice gestured acceptance with a grateful nod from the shoulders, but I wasn't feeling good about it—not at all. I would have been happier if she had refused my suggestions so I could call it quits. I had nagging doubts; I kept telling myself, "I'm not being professional, this guy's dangerous, tell her and end it." But I didn't.

I never sat down or let go of the leash, while acting as casual and relaxed as humanly possible for somebody who wouldn't sit down. Leaning against different walls, against the fake fireplace mantel with my arm draped across the mantelpiece, I started to get Daniel to do my bidding. I bantered with Eunice, wanting to keep all vibrations light and fluffy.

"First thing," I said to Eunice. "After my initial experience with him, I've decided to rename him. For me, anyhow, his name is Mister Daniel." And with Eunice bantering back I headed for another perch to drape my body on, requiring Mr. Daniel to come along. "Daniel, come," I said a little firmly, and with hardly a pull on the leash he was trotting across the room with me. When I got to the other side, I said "Sit." He sat. I said "Thank you." I told him "Stay," and stepped a few steps away to pick up my coffee cup. He stayed. Great.

We talked some more. Eunice, with a twinkle in her eye, was saying something about my having no right to change her dog's name, but since she liked the change she might allow it. Daniel was sitting. I faced him, said "Stay," and headed back to the coffee table to put my cup down.

The cup never made it. It's funny how through the corner of my eye the first thing I saw was the tail whip. No growl, no sound, no indication other than the tail whip, instantly followed by a leaping attack.

Escaping injury with much sweat, and without too much damage to Eunice's furniture, I got Daniel to stop aggressing with my passive resistance by preventing him from biting me but not correcting him. It took a long time, or at least seemed to, and Eunice's screaming and yelling didn't help. I was now drenched in sweat as I handed the leash to Eunice and told her to put Mr. Daniel in another room and make sure the door was securely closed. This enabled me to sit down for the first time in two hours and get myself together, because after this second trauma I was now totally exhausted.

It was this second attack that prompted me to say, "Eunice, I don't want anyone to be able to say that I was taking money training a dog that should have been put down. Therefore, I'll work with you for no charge. I'll take on the challenge for free under the following condition."

Eunice crossed her arms across her chest and said, "What condition?"

"Eunice," I said. "This is America, land of litigation. I read somewhere that there are more lawyers in this country than in the whole world put together. I want you to sign a memo of understanding acknowledging my stipulation that in order to keep the public safe, Daniel will always be muzzled when in the presence of anyone other than you. No matter how careful anyone is," I explained. "There's always human error, be it walking a dog or the Indian Point nuclear facility. By protecting the public, you will also protect yourself, me, and Daniel."

To my great astonishment she said, "I won't sign something like that." Actually, I was more than astonished. I was shocked at her refusal. "Well, that's the best I can do, Eunice. Think about it and get back to me if you change your mind."

Epilogue

No call ever came. I thought about Daniel and Eunice a lot over the next week. I seriously considered calling her to say that I'd work with her even if she didn't sign the agreement, as long as she promised me she would always muzzle him. After all, she was one of the good guys; she had rescued many dogs. I liked her and she really needed the help, and given enough time, patience, and effort, dogs like that can often be rehabilitated. Had I been younger, without three kids, I'm sure I would have made the call. It was probably fortunate that she never called. Every year, several times a year, a referring vet lays the "hard decision" on me. "I'm not telling you to put the dog down because of her aggression," the vet probably says to the dog owner. "Call Shelby. He'll tell you the truth, if it's manageable or not." Without fail, I warn the dog owners of the liability before helping them manage their dog's aggressive tendencies toward non-family members and/or other dogs. My red line is when the aggression is truly dangerous and directed toward family members. If the dog gets possessive-aggressive over a dropped baby back rib but is otherwise happy to share toys and is fine at the food bowl, it's manageable and not "truly serious." I remember a truly serious case in which a sixty-pound mixed breed didn't allow a family to enjoy breakfast, lunch, or dinner unless the people-food was shared with her. Her demanding growls were deadly serious and either met with tossed food from the table or bloodshed. The whole family was intimidated and walked on eggshells around this dog to avoid the myriad situations that caused aggressive responses. In this case, there was a clear danger to the family. Another consideration is the size of the dog. There's more flexibility when evaluating an aggressive sixteen-pound dog than a sixty-pound one. With more than 800 training appointments a year, half for behavioral problems, four or five times a year I have a terrible day where I have to advise a family to euthanize their dog. Yet, truth be told, I almost always feel the family's relief that the final terrible decision didn't have to be made by them, but by an expert.

PART 4

TURMOIL AT THE DOOR

U nless trained or too old to care, there's hardly a dog alive that isn't way too intrusive at the door. This ill-mannered behavior is actually connected to one of the key reasons man and dog bonded thousands of years ago: territoriality. Dogs served even then as they do today as alarm systems and protectors.

CHAPTER 12

CAN I TEACH MY DOG TO CONTAIN HIS ENTHUSIASM WHEN GREETING GUESTS?

Canines' incredible hearing and scenting makes it virtually impossible for somebody to enter a home undetected if there's a dog in the house. That coupled with territorial aggression is why you usually hear barking whenever you ring the bell of a dog owner. While most dogs will alert their owners that somebody's on the property or at the door, their follow-up response can vary widely. While the golden retriever's likely response is "Hi! Great to see you! Wanna throw a ball and play?" or "Here's the fridge, wanna share something?" the Doberman's response might be, "You ain't crossing the threshold without higher-up clearance!"

The basics of my dog training almost always include a "door turmoil routine," a routine at the door to eliminate the aggression or whatever unwelcome behavior the dog presents such as jumping or barking. And that lesson is usually one of the last lessons, because it requires redirecting a hardwired instinctual behavior, which isn't easy. Before the door routine can be established, the dog needs to be pretty efficient at the basics: coming, lying down, not jumping, respecting the word "quiet," and most important, using self-control by *staying* when told.

Start by teaching the dog not to jump on people unless invited to do so. This can be done in a multitude of ways:

If your dog is off leash, when his paws touch you, turn away from him with a shrug and scowl as you say "off."

If your dog is on leash, correct with a leash correction. The leash must be slack until the moment the front paws leave the floor. Immediately give the leash a light jerk to the side, accompanied by the word "off." As opposed to jerking back, a side jerk avoids impact and pressure on your dog's trachea.

You want to produce a sharp noise that startles the dog when his paws come off the ground. This strategy is a bit tricky as you have to be fast and the timing is critical. It can be a sound you produce yourself or with a device. Anything that your dog finds unpleasant while his front paws are off the ground or on you can be effective for curtailing the jumping.

The split second four paws are back on the floor, your dog needs to know that you're pleased, which should be a smile and a soft "good boy." Jumping up and down with boisterous loud praise is not necessary here. Timing is critical, though. Good training is not just about correcting unwanted behavior but, more importantly, about rewarding the wanted behavior. It's crucial to contrast the two. When his paws are on you, you're not happy, and it's not so pleasant for him; when he's off, you're happy.

The next step is teaching your dog the command, "Stay." When I say "stay," my arm is outstretched toward the dog with a flat hand, like a cop stopping traffic. More often than not, I can teach a dog to stay by just using my body language and the word "uh-uh" with a frown on my face. I make myself rigid, stiff and as big as can be, swelled up so to speak. After the command, the split second the dog starts to move, I step toward him saying "uh-uh," which almost always stops the dog cold, at which point I'm smiling and softly saying "good boy." I never use the word "no," because by the time I get there, most of the dogs think their name is "No Bad Dog!"

At this point, the focus is on increasing three things: the length of time he stays, the distance you can get away from him while he stays, and the intensity of the distraction through which he stays. Again, that's why my door turmoil routine lesson is usually one of the later lessons. The dog has to be pretty well trained for him to work through the distraction of the territorial response of someone at the door.

A good way to work on the door turmoil routine is to have a family member leave the house and return after a few minutes, knocking or ringing the bell. (Many dogs will act like they haven't seen you in months when you return after ninety seconds of putting out the garbage.) Make sure your dog is wearing his leash, although no one should be holding it.

Step 1: Thank your dog for alerting you to someone at the door, tell the "guest" to wait a second while you lure your dog away from the door with a treat, and tell him to "sit" and "stay," at which point he gets the first treat.

Step 2: Answer the door, but your real focus remains on your dog. Don't open the door unless he holds the "stay." If you

(Continued on next page)

have to pick up the dragging leash and bring him back to the spot away from the door multiple times, so be it.

Step 3: When you can open the door, keep it low-key with the "guest," so your dog is less likely to come rushing forward. When ready, tell him "Okay," and make sure he sees you have another treat to give him when he sits, as opposed to molesting the "guest." If done often enough, he should lose his enthusiasm with the same "guest" at the door and start to develop a politer greeting habit.

If potential aggression is an issue at the door, here's a good way to eliminate much of the dominant territorial response. More often than not, having visitors already in the house before the dog meets them eliminates a great deal of the aggressive territorial response. Have your dog out of sight when visitors arrive, preferably outside but if that's not an option then in another room. Let the dog in when the guests are seated at a table. Do not seat your guest on a couch or low-level piece of furniture; this leaves the guest vulnerable and the dog more confident and dominant, with his feet in your guest's lap and his face in your guest's face. You don't want the dog looking down on your guest and feeling like he's in command of the situation.

Until your dog really has it, every time a family member comes home, he or she should knock or ring the bell, and the person who is home should do the door turmoil routine. If you wait for real guests, it won't work. This door routine requires consistency to overcome a dog's natural territorial response. If door turmoil continues, I suggest investing in the help of a pro to help you get the dog under control and enhance your quality of life.

CHAPTER 13

HOW DO I KEEP MY DOG FROM JUMPING ALL OVER ME WHEN I COME HOME?

What do you do when there's no one home to do the aforementioned "door turmoil routine" with your dog? This is indeed a conundrum. Not too long ago, to avoid waking up the whole house, I told my daughter and son-in-law to leave their front door unlocked because I would be arriving from the airport around 2:00 a.m. Had I stood at the door fumbling with a key, their two dogs and my Paula Jean would have awoken the whole neighborhood with their barking. I approached the house quietly, opened the door quickly, and immediately greeted them using their names. There was one bark, and nobody, including my grandson, woke up.

First, your dog has to be taught not to jump on you unless invited to do so. This can be done in a multitude of ways. As soon as Jumper's paws touch you, turn away with a shrug and scowl as you say "off." You can also produce a startling noise with a whistle, anything that produces a sound that the dog finds unpleasant, while his front paws are on you. The split second four paws are on the floor, Jumper needs to know that you're pleased, which can be as subtle as a smile and a soft "good boy."

Timing is critical, as is consistency. When Jumper's paws are on you, you're not happy, and it's not so pleasant for him; when he's off, you're happy. When he doesn't jump, praise him verbally. If this strategy doesn't succeed, another you can employ is redirection. Make sure a drag leash and treats are within easy reach as you step through the door. A drag leash has no handle so it's less likely to get caught on anything while it's dragging and allows you to correct your dog without having to grab him by the scruff or collar. Your hands should only go to your dog for love and praise, petting and massaging. Grab both the drag leash and treats immediately as you tell Jumper to sit. While he's seated, give him a treat and attach the leash. Drop the leash and put your foot on it, keeping it loose. You want enough give so that if your dog jumps, he will hit the end of the leash halfway up, correcting himself for the inappropriate greeting. As he hits the end of the leash, frown and say "off." As soon as your dog's four paws are back on the floor, smile and say "thank you." Contrast! Remember, it's not just about correcting unwanted behavior but letting your dog know the behavior that you like. At this point, you should be able greet him calmly.

Sometimes leaving a leash and treats by the door is not possible. Every household needs to find what works for them. This may just be a case when having your dog "go hunting" allows you to enter your home unmolested. Just remember that you don't want to condition Jumper to expect treats every time he jumps on you, so it's important to make him earn it. Have your dog sit and stay for a minute, then toss one or two treats into the home and tell him "okay, go hunt!" While your dog is hunting, you can hang your coat and put on a pot of tea.

Whichever strategy you employ, make sure that everyone living in your household consistently displays a zero-tolerance attitude toward any jumping when they enter the home. Most dogs will choose to want to please you and comply.

CHAPTER 14

HOW DO I PREVENT MY DOG ESCAPING?

The answer? The "passive threshold routine." To me, the key value of these routines is *safety*. What would your dog do if you left the front door to your house or apartment open? Or a side or back door? What would your guess be as to the percentage of dogs that would immediately exit? How many of them would stay within sight of the house as opposed to those that would send you a postcard from another state, if they are lucky enough not to be killed by a car? How about those of you who resemble the Archie Bunker-Mike Stivic "squeeze jams" at the door, but it's with your dog "Pushy" competing to get out the door first?

The "passive threshold routine" is totally different from the "regular door routine." In the "regular door routine," when people come to visit and are at the door knocking, Pushy should be praised for telling you "somebody's on the verge of entering our den" with his barking at the door. Pushy should then be directed to go to his "spot" (which is away from the door) and then told "down" followed by "stay." The guests should then be let in and not molested by Pushy because he is laying down and staying at his spot. After the initial people-greetings at the door, Pushy is told "okay" at which point he's allowed to come and sit politely while greeting the guests. This is a great routine, because besides being civil at the door, it helps set a tone of good manners for the rest of the guests' visit. The "passive threshold routine" has nothing to do with guests, but rather with teaching Pushy never to cross any designated threshold without your permission. That threshold can be any house door, the porch, yard gate, car door, even the curb—any border that you identify. Pushy shouldn't cross it unless he hears the word "okay."

The "passive routine" should eliminate Pushy scooting out if there's a revolving door of kids or grandkids in your home running in and out all day (how many times have you yelled "Close the door!"). Same goes for the porch or car. Let's say you're hanging out on the porch with Pushy and decide to walk away to get the paper. You should be able to hop down the steps and walk away, and Pushy should stay on the porch without you saying anything. That's why it's passive; you don't command him to stay as you leave—he does it automatically. Same with the car; you should be able to open the door without Pushy hopping out after you until he hears you say "okay." In addition to my own dog, I've taught quite a few dogs in Manhattan not to leave a curb and enter a street until they hear the proverbial, "okay." When I lived in Queens, New York, my pharaoh hound Cheeta-Ann jogged off leash with me from my apartment to Fort Totten. We probably crossed a dozen streets. While I kept running if no cars were coming, Cheets automatically stopped at every curb. I could be as far as half a block away before I yelled out "okay," at which point she'd dash across and catch up.

Teaching a dog the passive routine is actually pretty easy. The hard part is the "forever" consistency. Let's say Pushy is on leash and we are at the threshold of the slider door to your yard, the front door, back door, porch door, yard gate, anywhere you don't want him to leave or cross without permission. With the leash slack and without saying anything, walk out and pop the leash while saying "uh-uh" the split second Pushy is crossing the threshold to follow you. This will cause him to stop dead at the threshold, waiting for you. A few seconds later, turn around and say "okay" at which point he should exit and you can give him a treat. When timed correctly, within just a few passes, Pushy should learn this new routine. If you want to have any chance for this cooperative behavior to be Pushy's habit, you have to enforce the passive routine every single time once it's taught. Every single time. This routine can save lives. *It's worth it.*

CHAPTER 15

HOW DO I PREVENT MY DOG FROM MENACING MY GUESTS WHEN THEY TRY TO LEAVE?

Years ago, someone told me that the guard dogs left in Macy's main store in New York were trained to let the thieves in, but not out. I have no idea if that's true of the Macy's dogs, but I've personally met dogs trained who do just that. Police patrol dogs are often taught to "hold a bad guy at bay" until the posse shows up.

Then, there are the canine "naturals." You're having some friends over for wine and pâté, or beer and chips, and at the end of the night, it's time for the guests to leave. Your dog, with no training whatsoever, attacks your unsuspecting guest who has been petting the dog all night, for having the audacity to leave. This would be a good thing if the dog was assisting you in the course of an arrest, but it's the last thing in the world you need when entertaining friends.

Over the years, I've met several of these problematic "naturals." I remember an insurance salesman whose good-size dog named Bob grabbed his tie (while he was wearing it) and wouldn't let go. His wife had to come downstairs to put a leash on the dog, and walk them all outdoors, with the guy bent over at a ninety-degree angle, while Bob held on to the tie and continued growling just eight inches from his owner's face. That's when I got called. The owners told me it started with Bob circling and barking at anybody trying to leave and getting more and more aggressive about people leaving over time. Bob's type of separation anxiety was pretty hardwired by this time, so in addition to basic training, I worked to break a habitual bad routine and replace it with a better one for people's departure that should work for you, too. Ten minutes before anyone planned to leave, Bob was lured to a spot with a view of the door, leashed to an eyehook in the molding, and given a hollow marrow bone with a piece of meat wedged in the middle. It took about two weeks until Bob ran to his tie-down spot and looked forward to Dad's leaving for work.

For many years, I did presentations for the Hug-a-Tree and Survive program that teaches children how to survive in the woods should they become lost. As part of my presentation, I would introduce them to my partner, search dog Michelle, who I told them was more valuable than 400 people searching thanks to her scenting ability and training. I then had her perform some tricks, including pretending to drop down dead when I shot her with my fingers held in the shape of a gun. It was always a crowd pleaser. At the end of the presentation, the children would come over and pet the "dangerous Doberman" who they discovered was a friendly sweetheart.

At ninety pounds, my dog Michelle could have won this tug of war in a second but didn't because she enjoyed the game so much. The growling while tugging sounded like two lions wanting to kill each other. Sometimes the rope would slip out of my other dog Tri's mouth, but Michelle would shove it back in his face so they could keep playing.

My apprentice Jeremy and his two dogs paddleboarding in the middle of the harbor, something a lot of dog owners would love to do with their dogs. The dogs had to be trained to get on the board, stay on the board, and enjoy the water. Playing water sports together and everyone having a great time—a perfect example of harmony.

Kelsey the pit bull mix harmoniously sharing her bed with one of her two-legged significant others, my grandson Jasper. These two are definitely BFFs.

© Tom Shelby

Predatory aggression has a strong genetic component. My Doberman Mike would have eaten these birds in a heartbeat, yet my other Doberman Michelle (pictured here) would stand under their cage and whine, indicating that she wished to play with them. Clearly, the birds loved her.

The question is, "Who is imitating whom?"

Not posed. Just hanging out in harmony. My wife, Jaye, my grandson, Jasper, and I along with Paula Jean (my poodle on the floor), Foster (my son Brett's dog that he fostered and kept, sitting next to Jasper), and Kelsey (my daughter Kerry's dog).

Sometimes I would want to take Michelle and Tri to a park where they could run free, but it was too far away to walk, so my four-legged kids would hop into the bicycle trailer designed for two-legged kids. They were cooperative and stayed in the trailer regardless of distractions until we reached the park and were told they could come out.

© Tom Shelby

Helicopters are very loud and produce enormous vibrations that can be uncomfortable and scary to dogs. During Mike's search and rescue training, he was acclimated to helicopters so that he and I could work alongside and with air search teams.

© Tom Shelby

Just a guy chilling out with two dogs, right? Wrong! My brilliant friend Broderick, who has multiple PhDs, was frightened of big dogs. Mike and MacDuff, two very well-mannered dogs, befriended him and helped him overcome his fear. In the event that Broderick's parents didn't believe him, he asked me to take this picture as proof.

When I first met Roxie as a puppy to help with her training, I kept calling her Roxie Girl for some reason. The name stuck as she matured into a beautiful and sweet companion, so sweet that she became a pediatric therapy dog at Morgan Stanley Children's Hospital. Thank you, Roxie Girl.

© Tom Shelby

Contrary to my objections, the kids shared lunch with Michelle in my homemade igloo.

© Tom Shelby

Although often perceived as fierce, Dobbies have a soft and cuddly side like all other dogs—my Mikey was no exception.

Every chance we get, my Paula Jean and I go hiking. Here she is enjoying the beautiful view from the top of Black Rock Mountain in New Jersey.

Not long after I got married, my wife and I brought home the first addition to our family, Cheeta-Ann. In this picture, she's still a puppy. I named her Cheeta-Ann because she was the absolute fastest dog I had ever seen.

© Tom Shelby

Not a fight. Michelle is just roughhousing with one of her best friends, Abu. Both were excellent search and rescue dogs.

© Tom Shelby

Best friends Mike (Doberman) and MacDuff (miniature pinscher) resting after a short hike to Jetty Beach, Martha's Vineyard. People used to say I should call them Me and Mini-Me.

© Tom Shelby

True harmony. A beautiful sail with Michelle and Tri.

Harmony comes in many forms. I worked with one of Jeremy's dogs, Reggie (terrier mix), on basic behavior. He is smarter than some of my friends.

Mycroft was so smart and learned so quickly that if he had decided to go to college he would have been accepted by Harvard.

Valjean, at the point in his training where he would cooperate without his owners having to hold his leash.

PART 5

SOCIALIZING A DOG

Socialize! This is critically important. The most stable dog is afraid of nothing, so if they are exposed to everything and nothing bites them, their attitude becomes "Been there, done that, seen that, no big deal!" That's what you want! If Main Street and 18-wheelers don't scare them, other dogs, babies, and squirrels shouldn't faze them.

CHAPTER 16

HOW DO I MAKE SURE MY DOG HAS FUN AT THE DOG PARK?

I've been waiting a long time for this question; looking forward to addressing it. I've worked with a lot of dogs at a lot of dog parks over the years in New York and New Jersey. To me, watching dogs interact is better than watching TV. With a discerning eye, it can be quite educational. I was asked to speak at a National Search and Rescue Conference several years ago where one of the presenters showed a forty-minute video of dogs playing at a dog park. Based on the "mode" of play exhibited by the individual dogs, their personalities were discussed in detail. What could be garnered from "how they play" was amazing.

Some years ago, I was at a dog park in NYC located on the East Side, literally hanging over the East River. Great spot to watch the boat and helicopter traffic while the dogs do their thing. I was there with a client and her Brittany spaniel, and before we went through the double gates to enter the run, I zeroed in on a Lab's body language as he went after a ball that his owner threw. The Lab was clearly stressed with the competition for the ball, and I became even more stressed knowing that Bonnie, the Brittany, loves chasing balls, so I didn't unhook her from the leash as the Lab-owner tossed the ball again. On this throw, a wirehair fox terrier got to the ball first, and the Lab attacked, killing the terrier before anyone could prevent it.

Out of my eight hundred training appointments per year, about half were for behavioral problems, and the worst had to do with aggression. In the case of the Lab in the park, it was a clear case of possessive aggression or resource guarding, the resource being the ball. My recommendation is to leave the toys at home. When you are at the gate of the park, take a quick look to make sure there's no Cujo (dog who looks stressed) in the dog park. Bottom line, if you don't like what you see, pass.

In my opinion, dog parks are a great place to socialize dogs. Just like your child's experience in nursery school, the dog park is an opportunity for your dog to socialize and learn how to get along with multiple personalities and ethnicities i.e. French bulldog, Afghan hound, English setter, Japanese Shiba Inu, Mexican Chihuahua, or Rhodesian ridgeback. The dog run is really a mini United Nations. You want your dog to have lots of positive interactions with as many dogs as possible in order to be a confident, happy dog.

CHAPTER 17

DOGS AND BABIES AND TODDLERS AND KIDS. WHAT DO I NEED TO KNOW?

Even if a person from a small town who's never gone any-where sees a traveling circus pass through his town with an elephant and a clown doing cartwheels, he won't be shocked or frightened. Not so for our four-legged friends. Even the most socialized dogs are likely to at least "alert" if not growl or run from something they have never seen. I've had several clients over the years ask me why their dogs growl at homeless people. "Because they act, and often smell, quite different from what your dog is accustomed to," I answer. So, if your well-socialized dog never saw a one-year-old baby learning to walk with what I call the "Frankenstein lurch," depending on the dog, he may growl in fear to stop this strangely approaching little person—or not. My dog Cheeta-Ann had no problem with my daughter Tara when she was crawling on top of her of her bed or learning to walk. Later, when my other children Kerry and Brett played house and dressed Cheeta in everything from jewelry to hats, Cheeta loved the attention.

Even if you do everything right in the introduction of your dog to babies, toddlers, or five-year-olds, it very well may depend on the dog's genetics when it comes to young two-legged. You, as the dog owner, have to be hyper vigilant in the observation of your dog's response to kids of all ages. Be it the puppy that plays too roughly with a two-year-old or the five-year-old rescue you took off death row, there's no pat answer to get your dog to love kids. If you have no idea how your adult rescue is with kids, start at the nearest grade school at three o'clock when the kids get out and see how Saver responds to the running and yelling kids. If he seems relaxed, have a kid offer Saver some treats. If that works, next stop is nursery school when it lets out.

I'm a "depends" trainer, so my observation of a dog's response to the "inappropriate" or "different" behavior of toddlers determines my training response. If your dog is nervous with toddlers, perhaps start with preteens, having them offer your Saver treats, slowly working your way down to younger and younger kids. When it comes to kids and dogs, if not sure, err on the side of safety. If necessary, your dog may need to be told "Leave it" if kids are running past. Remember, the "Leave it" command ensures that your dog will "leave" anything—a trash can, fallen ice cream cone, raccoon, and a person, too. Or, you may need to say to the two-leggeds, "No, not very friendly, please don't pet."

So, here's the rub. *The kids* themselves! I remember being in a friend's house and his six-year-old daughter was in an adjoining room with my sweet little Cavalier King Charles spaniel Tri. All of a sudden, Tri cried out in pain. As we rushed into the room, the little girl jumped back saying, "I didn't do anything to hurt him!" So, here's the truth: the other thing that requires your close observation is how the baby, toddler, or child interacts with the puppy or older dog. Babies tend to grab everything and anything and hold on tight. Some dogs won't appreciate having their ears pulled or sucked on by a baby. Saver may be great in all respects with your four-year-old girl, except when he's chewing on a favorite toy, and even though you told her to leave him alone when he's busy with it, she may not listen, or just forget.

Bottom line? There are no set rules here. It depends on a dog's genetics and experience with kids. And it depends on the age and temperament of the child. When it comes to mixing kids and dogs, *it's on you.* Observe and act accordingly.

CHAPTER 18

WHAT'S THE BEST WAY TO INTRODUCE MY DOG TO OTHER DOGS WHEN WE'RE OUT FOR A WALK?

If you're asking this question, it can only mean you have some apprehension about meeting dogs when you're out for a walk with yours. Your concern could be caused by a myriad of things. Perhaps your dog gets overly excited at the prospect of making a new friend and that makes you nervous and just that little bit embarrassed. Perhaps your dog has experienced some dog-related trauma and is now aggressive or overly cautious when encountering new dogs. In either case, I have some strategies that should help your excursions outside become pleasant once again for both you and your dog.

What do you do when your dog's unfettered joy and bliss at seeing possible playmates becomes an unhinged frenzied response, and the ensuing embarrassment totally destroys your happy, relaxed walk? On a couple of occasions, my wife has threatened to hire a dog trainer to help her stop our dog Paula Jean from embarrassing her by jumping straight up in the air and barking when she sees another person also walking a dog on a leash. (Perhaps a slight case of the shoemaker's kids needing new soles?) If a dog's life is basically the house and backyard, it's not unusual to get a *holy cow* crazy response to another dog walker coming toward you. Your dog needs to learn some self-restraint, and that comes from learning manners.

Upon seeing another dog, don't try to make Boisterous Betty sit and stay. Having Boisterous Betty sit and stay while another dog is approaching is equivalent to me telling you to sit on the railroad track as the train is approaching. The closer the other dog gets, the more your dog is being whipped into a frenzy. Keep moving but draw her attention to you with a happy voice and treats (people-food treats). This is also a good time to use the "Look at me" command (explained in detail in Part 3), which will redirect Boisterous Betty's attention, keeping her eyes locked on you. She can also be told to "Leave it" (explained in detail in Part 8) and then "Heel." A dog should walk away for any object, animal, or person, no matter how tantalizing, when she hears you say "Leave it!" Like "Look at me," the "Heel" command can be considered a form of redirection. When your dog is heeling, she is essentially glued to your left knee and never wanders from there. Whether you're walking slowly, running, making sudden stops, whatever, she's at your left knee. You can learn more about "Heel" in Part 3. With these commands, you are taking control of the potential encounter and, if you want, mandating that your dog not insist on meeting this other dog or person. If so inclined, when within earshot, you can ask the other leash holder if his dog is friendly, and, only if all are amenable, allow for the proverbial meet-and-greet.

On the other end of the spectrum is the dog who was traumatized and has good reason to be suspicious of any new dog. First and foremost, read the other dog! If the other dog looks relaxed, has a stupid-looking slack-jaw grin with soft eyes and a wagging tail, go ahead and approach. If you're looking at a dog with a stiff stance, hard eyes, a stiff tail not wagging or tucked under between his legs (fearful), and growling, then pass. Regardless of what you observe, ask every person you see on the other end of the leash, in no uncertain terms, "Is your dog friendly?" If the answer has any hesitancy or uncertainty whatsoever, pass. If the answer is, "Usually," or "Most of the time," or "I think so," pass. Have your dog heel and tell him to leave it if necessary. If, on the other hand, the answer is "Very friendly," encourage your dog to meet this new potential friend.

It's important to guard against inadvertently transferring your anxiety to your dog. Picture this probably familiar scene: a half a block away, there's a person coming straight toward you with his dog on leash. Anticipating your dog's discomfort, your mounting anxiety causes you to tighten the leash while nervously saying "Nelly!" Having only said the name, with no command or request given, all your dog hears is nervous energy and anxiety, and to what will she relate your tension and unease? The approaching dog, of course! Then, as she's fearfully hesitating or displaying aggressive behavior, you tell her, "It's okay," inadvertently rewarding her fear response. If your four-year-old child was frightened by the ghost at the door on Halloween, you could say, "It's okay, it's only a little boy under a sheet," and your kid would understand. But to a dog, it's all about body language, voice intonation, and timing. Your response to a dog's actions, *as the actions are happening*, is what teaches a dog. The physicality of tightening the leash (body language) and anxiously saying her name (voice intonation) increases her concern as she's looking at the approaching dog. Rewarding her fear by saying, "It's okay" (voice intonation) results in the inadvertent cause and rewarding of unwanted behavior.

So, what to do when you see an approaching dog? From now on, I suggest you have treats with you whenever you go out with Nelly. I wouldn't be averse to people-food treats if the only time she got them was just before meeting new dogs. Without tightening the leash, the moment the other four-legged is visible, express your unmitigated joy and happiness through your voice at the possible "new best friend" your dog is about to meet, not to mention the treats you're giving her to further her happiness at seeing the possible "new friend." As soon as the other dog comes into view, your voice intonation is expressing your exuberance and elation: "Look at that, Nelly! That may become your new best friend! Isn't that great?" You never sounded so happy in your life as you're calling out to the approaching leash holder, "Friendly?" The purpose of your wildly happy tone and treats is to tell Nelly that meeting new dogs is a good thing. If you get a "Yes, very," answer to the "Friendly" question, keep walking, don't stop, and let Nelly do her thing, kind of. Keep the leash soft and talk happily to all, and keep the meeting short, because you want success to build on success. If she wants to have a sniff session with the new dog, great! Stay low-key and happy, give it a few seconds, and say "time to go," leading her away with a "heel," and with treats if you want. If she turns back, add a "leave it." Even if she's having a good time with her new acquaintance, leave the scene with her wanting more rather than staying too long. The new friend might get too comfortable, even pushy, and start making Nelly feel uncomfortable. A short encounter guarantees a successful meeting with a stranger, and may even leave her wanting more, which is what you want.

If Nelly pulls hard and wants to create a space wide enough to fit the Pentagon between her and the other dog, don't let her! I'm not saying try to force her to meet Mr. Friendly, but rather continue on walking by while keeping up a positive, upbeat chatter. If the leash actually goes slack as she stops trying to pull away, add some treats to the happy talk. Her confidence will increase as she has more and more experience being in the presence of and socializing with newcomers.

CHAPTER 19

IS THERE A GOOD WAY TO BRING MY DOG TO VISIT FAMILY THAT ALSO HAS A DOG?

When a friend introduces me to a new friend of his, my expectation is one of mutual respect and pleasant conversation as we get to know each other. It's not quite the same with dogs. Without any kind of introduction, two young puppies meeting for the first time may immediately dive into wild play and roughhousing as though they were from the same litter. Two one-year-old dogs meeting for the first time are more likely to be more cautious; a little sniffing to see if the other comes up to snuff, then they may play, or not. Adult dogs usually behave in a similar way. Generally speaking, dogs meeting off leash are more likely to be tolerant or friendlier than dogs on leash, connected to a person. A well-socialized dog is also more likely to have easier and more relaxed encounters. Just picture the Manhattan dog that sees other four-leggeds of all breeds and sizes every day on its walks as compared to his suburban counterpart whose response is "Holy cow" on the occasional sighting of another dog being walked.

Let's say you get a call from your sister who lives two hours away.

"Thanksgiving at my house this year," she says. "And, by the way, I just adopted a male two-year-old Shepherd mix named Homey . . . just so you know when you bring Jet for the long weekend."

Your next question should be, "How does Homey get along with other dogs?"

"Okay, I guess. He's met a few dogs and it was okay." If you weren't too confident in your sister's response about Homey, and you know that Jet on occasion has been sketchy with other dogs, ask Sis to rub Homey's face with a small rag and send it to you. You do the same with Jet and send it back to Sis. When you get Homey's rag, put it under Jet's bed, just as Jet's odiferous rag should be placed under Homey's bed. Hopefully, the other dog's mild scent will be well received, as it should be associated with a very positive place to a dog: his bed. The dogs' actual first meeting should be away from the house, ideally off leash in a large open area. If that's not convenient, have a casual on-leash meeting. After the proverbial sniffing, take a fifteen-minute walk together back to the house, with Jet entering Homey's house first. All talk should be upbeat and happy.

Let's say your buddy who lives a short walk or car drive away calls and says, "Hey man, just got a new dog named Fresh. Let's get 'em together." The meeting should be similar to Homey and Jet's, except here you don't need to exchange the "scent rags." Instead, casually meet in neutral territory. If the dogs can't be off leash, take a nice long walk ending up at one of your houses. Keep it upbeat and happy and don't overstay the visit. Separate them when they're having a good time, making it more likely that they'll harmonize during your next get-together.

CHAPTER 20

HOW DO I INTRODUCE MY DOG TO MY NEW BABY?

The mission here is to create sibling harmony as opposed to sibling rivalry between your dog and new baby. Many owners worry that their dog, who may very well have been the family's first baby, will feel neglected and act out with the arrival of this new "sibling." Having three children of my own, I've experienced coming home from the hospital and making the dog-newborn introductions. Luckily, our dog Cheeta was a natural when it came to kids. Nonetheless, my wife Jaye and I created positive olfactory associations for Cheeta prior to our babies coming home and went out of our way to share with her as many interactions as possible with our babies. To Jaye and me, these were revered as very special times for our immediate family. Yet, to my surprise (and slight discomfort), I've been asked about half a dozen times to be a part of the reception crew when Mom and new baby were arriving home from hospital, so here's what I suggest to break the ice. Assuming you are not coming home the same day you give birth, gently rub the baby all over with two pieces of cloth or take two articles of clothing the baby wore for a few hours and have someone place one under the dog's food bowl and the other under where your dog sleeps. Where a dog eats and sleeps are two very positive places for a dog and should give her a positive association to the scent of the baby. When it comes time for the actual introduction, with a loving, soft tone, invite your dog to smell the baby's feet, and give her a very special treat that includes people food.

From that point on, whenever you feed, change diapers, or interact with the baby in any way, call your dog over and give her treats to share the experience. Many new parents inadvertently do the opposite, creating jealousy. "Not now, dog, I have to feed the baby!" Or, "Not now, I have to 'whatever' the baby." You want to include your dog in activities having to do with the baby. Even though you will still do things alone with your dog, try to spend your quality time with dog and baby together. Bring the baby along to the dog park and for walks. This way you're making the dog and the baby a kind of team, creating the harmony you want.

CHAPTER 21

SHOULD I LET MY DOG PLAY ROUGH WITH OTHER DOGS?

When dogs play, they chase each other and play-fight, and more often than not, to the distress of many owners, verbalize when playing. When my Doberman Michelle played tug-of-war using a rope toy with my other dog Tri, it was a ninety-pound Doberman against a seventeen-pound Cavalier King Charles spaniel. She could have easily ripped it out of Tri's mouth, but didn't because she enjoyed the game, and you should have heard the decibel level of the growling coming from both of them! To Michelle and Tri, as with many other dogs, playing included growling. Michelle and her best friend, a shepherd mix named Daisy, spent many years playing and hiking together. Whey they played, they often sounded like two lions fighting to the death. And yet, on one occasion, play got out of hand for Michelle and Daisy. Their roughhousing got carried away and they got into an actual fight. It wasn't too hard to break up because they didn't really want to fight. It was mostly bluster. Human best friends have fights now and then too, don't they?

The judgment of who your dog plays with and how hard is on

your shoulders. You know your dog the best. What is his temperament and how easily can he become overly excited? What is his ability to take rough play and his threshold for getting unstrung and too aggressive? How well does he interact with other dogs? Play should always be a positive experience.

CHAPTER 22

HOW DO I GET MY DOG TO
STOP FREAKING OUT AT NEW SOUNDS
AFTER A BIG MOVE?

The most stable dog's attitude when out and about is, "Been there, done that, seen that, no big deal." You want your dog to be like the experienced world traveler who is relaxed and doesn't get fazed by much, but if you've moved from the quiet countryside to the city and Cruiser is experiencing a barrage of new and loud sounds including ear-piercing fire engines, screeching ambulances rushing by, and the crash-boom of garbage trucks collecting rubbish curbside, he's most likely freaking out. If you want Cruiser to be the jet-setting globetrotter of his new neighborhood, start by exposing him, on a positive basis, to a variety of sounds to help desensitize him to the more disturbing sounds. By positive basis, I mean that you want him to be aware of the sound, but not frightened by it.

When you and Cruiser are home in the apartment, as soon as you notice him cock his ears when he hears sirens or any other distressing sound in the distance, give him treats while happily telling him how fun those sounds are. Cruiser is less likely to be scared when he hears them up close. I've had many clients over the years play CDs of thunder, sirens, gunshots, explosions, short-pipe Harley motorcycles, etc., and play them loud enough to be heard, but not so loud as to frighten. As Cruiser hears these sounds he should be getting treats and praise, helping to desensitize him and make the sounds less scary.

CHAPTER 23

HOW DO I BUILD MY DOG'S CONFIDENCE?

How do you take an insecure dog and make him a confident dog? How do you make a coward brave? It's much harder to make a fearful dog confident than to take the overly confident dog down a notch or two. The most stable dog is afraid of nothing. You can teach a dog to be afraid of nothing by socializing him and exposing him, on a positive basis, to everything you can think of. Introduce him to healthy, friendly dogs, babies (of the human variety), dog-friendly cats, every imaginable sound he's eventually going to hear, and lots and lots of people. Many dogs bite out of fear, and since more than half of my training appointments have been with problem dogs, I've seen a lot of fear-biters, and plenty of dogs that were not biters, but nonetheless extremely fearful of anything new.

One summer, while visiting friends in New Jersey, my standard poodle, Paula Jean, and I came across a life-size statue of a cow. It was made out of some kind of plastic material and was so lifelike that Paula froze when she saw it and started emanating a low soft growl from her throat. It took me fifteen minutes of patient cajoling and praising every forward step until Paula would sniff the cow.

Not long after I adopted Paula Jean, I took her to a huge outdoor fair known as the AG, the Agriculture Fair. It was her first exposure to a multitude of farm animals, amusement rides, a gazillion people (many with dogs), and vendors hawking their wares. She was adapting well until a rock band near us seemed (to Paula Jean) to explode into music when they all of a sudden started playing after a break. Paula was so startled that she jumped straight up in the air and pulled to get as far away, as fast as possible. I did not take her home but instead spoke to her in an upbeat manner as we casually moved away from the band. When we were about fifty yards away, she was a lot more relaxed even though she could clearly still hear the music. I redirected her attention into earning some treats for a little obedience (OB) work: sit, stay, down, etc. We also played a little tug-of-war with a stick, which is often a good confidence builder. Being happy and playful with a little OB thrown in, I worked our way back to the band by redirecting her attention to me and having fun and treats while ignoring the music. We ended up standing in front of the band for their last couple of minutes playing, and the drummer was happy to give Paula a treat at my suggestion.

Dealing with fear is complicated. Saying "It's okay" and soothing your dog lovingly can end up seriously rewarding a fear response. The last thing you want to do is accidentally reward an unwanted behavior. Imagine you're walking down the street with your dog, a truck backfires, and the dog hits the end of the leash, shaking in fear. Most people will overly comfort their dogs, petting and kissing them excessively, saying "It's okay." Some will pick the dog up and carry him past the offending noise. Some will turn around and not go past the scary sound. If you do these things repeatedly with a fearful dog, you'll end up with a basket case, having rewarded the fear response. I experienced this very situation once when I was teaching a young GSP (German shorthaired pointer) to heel in Manhattan. The GSP freaked out, trying to go back the other way, refusing to pass the truck. With a little forced pulling and coaxing, we passed the truck by about thirty feet. With a pet on the head and in an animated voice, I smiled and said to the dog shaking in fear, "Hey, good boy! That was a fun! We're good to go!" Then, with gentle firmness, we continued again past the offending truck. The "good boy" supplies the comfort needed and passing the object without getting "bitten" is the confidence builder. When we turned around and went past it again, the GSP presented much less resistance. We did it again and again as he earned treats by casually walking by the "nasty truck."

Let's say your dog is terrified of the roar of passing airplanes. Look upward a lot to try to see the plane first (but be aware that she may hear it before you do, as a dog's hearing is far more acute than ours), at which point you should start praising her with great enthusiasm and feeding her people-food treats. This will give her a new, positive association with airplanes. Be very careful of your timing, though. If your dog starts showing fear, don't continue giving her treats. That would be rewarding her fear response. Instead, continue walking while remaining upbeat and enthusiastic. "Wow! Aren't those planes cool? Don't you wish you could fly, too?"

Some dogs are afraid of people visiting their home. They might bark or growl, get the shakes, release some urine, or run away to hide in other rooms or under furniture. In cases like this, when guests come over I suggest holding your dog's leash, which is attached to a harness, as you open the door and let your guests in. Both you and the guests should ignore your dog. Keep her close to you, though, basically forcing her to deal with the strangers in close proximity, but without the strangers actually confronting her.

That's how a good part of the visit is going to go. Whether your dog's leash is tied to a bureau leg in the area of activity or being held by you or one of the guests, the goal is for her to become desensitized to the presence of "aliens" in her home. This is a good time to add tiny pieces of meat to the equation. When she's not at the end of the leash, pulling to get away, offer her people food. If the only time she gets people food is in conjunction with new people and experiences, her fear is going to be lessened. I've used this approach successfully a thousand times. When feasible, have guests offer her the people-food treats and watch her become Miss-Happy-to-Meet-You.

A confident dog is more likely to be happy and face new people and experiences with a positive attitude. Left unresolved, a dog's fears can escalate to fear aggression, the extreme end of fear behavior. An awful lot of dogs have been euthanized simply because they were afraid, and that is frankly heartbreaking. Let me set the scene. Your dog Bashful is quite shy around people and other dogs, and, being your caring self, you don't want to stress him out so you go out of your way not to expose him to anything and anyone that could frighten him. One day, a friend and his puppy Cheery come over to your house with the hope of your two dogs becoming BFFs. Bashful is appalled and immediately hides under the bed, absolutely refusing to come out. What happens then? Bashful discovers that "the best defense is a good offense." When you reach under the bed to get Bashful out, for the first time ever he snaps at you and you recoil, the human body's automatic response. And that's a lesson you cannot undo! Bashful just discovered *that works! Threaten what scares or offends, and it retreats, it pulls back!* Without knowledgeable intervention, Bashful will become more and more aggressive, keeping any unwanted attention away with growls and teeth. I've met plenty of fear-aggressive dogs. Dogs that stepped in poop but won't let you touch their feet to clean—feet touching too scary. Dogs that won't let you remove an engorged tick, won't let a groomer or vet touch them, will bite rather than be removed from a closet or under a table. "The best defense is a good offense" list goes on and on. It is difficult to convert Bashful into Braveheart, and this is precisely why properly socializing is so important.

The goal here is to make your dog's attitude *been there, done that, seen that, no big deal.* I've helped dogs terrified of sewer grates, clanging flagpoles, a burned tree stump, a barber pole, stone lion statues, you name it. The most confident dog is afraid of nothing, and how do you get a dog afraid of nothing? You expose him to everything.

CHAPTER 24

WHAT ARE SOME GREAT GAMES TO PLAY WITH MY DOG?

Fred Rogers of the PBS show *Mister Rogers' Neighborhood* is known for saying that "play is often talked about as if it were a relief from serious learning. But for children play *is* serious learning." The same can said for our four-legged significant others. We engage in all kinds of play with our dogs and often they initiate the play—sometimes more than we want!

A favorite game of mine is a variation of "fetch." It's lots of fun for four-leggeds and two-leggeds alike, but also teaches the dog a potentially useful skill. To me, having a dog who will retrieve stuff on command is tremendous. Both my search dogs, Michelle and Michael, retrieved on request. I once dropped the cap of a pill bottle from the top of the steps and it fell to the first floor. I told Michelle, who was next to me, to "bring" the bottle cap. She wasn't familiar with the term "bottle cap," but had seen what just happened, zipped down the stairs, retrieved the cap, brought it back up, and dropped it in my hand. It was great in that it saved me the trip up and down the stairs, but not a one hundred percent success because of the dog saliva in the cap. Another time,

Michelle brought me the glove of a missing person during a search in the woods, and then had me follow her to where she found the glove! I name everything my dogs retrieve. It's called article discrimination. There's a border collie with a recorded ability to retrieve over one thousand items by name!

I remember teaching my dog Paula Jean to fetch and drop items on command. I made a show of grabbing a new toy off the floor, a plush toy frog with rope legs. I let her know I had treats in the other hand, at which point that hand went behind my back as I teased her with the frog. When she was trying to grab it from me, I threw it and said, "Fetch the frog." This is where patience is needed because Paula picked up the frog, shook it, ran around the house like an idiot, dropped it fifteen feet from where I was sitting on the couch, and then came to me for a treat. I smiled and softly said "Fetch Froggie" with no sign of impatience or frustration or sternness in my voice. Paula didn't bring the toy back, so I had to walk the fifteen feet, get Froggie myself, and start the process again several times. When she finally dropped it within reach of my position on the couch, she got a treat for the first time. Step by small incremental step, I got her to bring it closer and closer until she eventually dropped it directly in my hand. I taught her to "drop it" by holding a treat with one hand next to her nose and the other hand under her mouth as she dropped the toy to get the treat. The first few times she put Froggie in my hand, she got a jackpot, a few treats instead of one, and a minute of play and tug with the toy.

Having a search and rescue background, one of my favorite games is "go find!" When my children were in grade school, I was often asked to do canine demonstrations for their classmates. Some of my favorite memories are with my pharaoh hound Cheeta-Ann. She would sit in the hallway, just outside of the classroom, while I handed a Milk-Bone to one of the children in class with the instruction to hide the bone anywhere in the classroom. Once hidden, I would let Cheeta-Ann in and told her to "go find." She was always successful within a few minutes. Actually, on several occasions, she alerted on candy bars and half eaten sandwiches that students had hidden, which were certainly more interesting than the Milk-Bone. These finds were always met with laughter by both the students and their teacher.

I started teaching Paula to "go find" by making it clear to her that I had a Milk-Bone in my hand as I told her to sit and stay. I then backed away, acting a little silly, which piqued her attention. I then turned around, tossed a Milk-Bone across the room, and said enthusiastically, "Go find the bone!" She immediately found and devoured it. Remember, you want success to build on success. After this first find, I took Paula back to the original spot and had her sit and stay again. I backed up again, still acting a little silly, and placed the bone in the same area where the first one had been but out of sight this time, behind the couch, causing her to begin the transition from using sight to smell. I continued this game for about twenty minutes, making the biscuit more and more difficult to find each time. Like most dogs, Paula's enthusiasm was quite intense as she relished the challenge and reward of the find.

When a dog understands and loves the "go find" game, he can be trained to find anything: illegal drugs, bomb-making materials, missing people, and even cancer. It all starts with "go find." I've also found that the tug-of-war game can increase a dog's confidence, but it has to be done properly. With the somewhat shy dog, I feel it can augment his confidence because it elicits a playful aggressive response exhibited by the dog's growling and shaking of the item that is being tugged. If the dog has exhibited some possessive-aggressive behaviors, though, I only play the game if he will immediately release the tug item when I say "drop it." The dog has to understand that it is a game with rules. The happiest dogs in the world are the ones who earn your praise and joy. When you play with your dog, you're both strengthening your bond and making him or her smarter by the mental stimulation.

DOG TRAINING DIARY

MY FIRST CHILD: PHARAOH HOUND CHEETA-ANN

"If you pick up a starving dog and make him prosperous,
he will not bite you. That is the principal difference
between a dog and a man."
—Mark Twain

Cheeta-Ann was my family's first dog. Jaye and I were newly married when we got Cheeta-Ann. Like so many of my clients who got a dog before they had a child, Cheeta-Ann was our first "kid." Jaye and I originally agreed upon a Doberman breeder (who also bred pharaoh hounds) to pick out a puppy that would be ready to leave the litter in a week.

A week later, I came home with a pharaoh hound instead of the Doberman puppy we planned to get. I had never seen a pharaoh hound before and was completely taken aback by their beauty and grace. When the breeder regaled me with the breed's incredible intelligence, lack of health issues, intuitiveness, etc. I fell in love. Lo and behold, two puppies were available at the time, a male and a female. The breeder put them on the floor for me to observe for a while. I dropped a heavy book on the tile floor when they weren't looking to observe their response. I was hoping to see surprise followed by curiosity, which I did. The tile floor they were on was white with black designs, and I noticed the female was keenly aware when she crossed from white to black and vice versa. I was blown away with what I considered an unbelievably sensitive awareness for a twelve-week-old puppy. "I'll take her," I said, and I did.

I later learned that great sensitivity in a dog isn't necessarily "great." You should have seen the spectacle Cheeta made of herself whenever she had to walk from a dock to a boat. The spaces between the dock's wooden planks revealed a ten-foot drop to the water, which Cheeta found totally unacceptable and would express her concern by screaming at the decibel level of an ambulance. I would then lift her up and carry her to the middle of the dock, but when I put her down she would scream again and flatten herself in the down position. I'm sure many behaviorists will say I did the absolutely wrong thing; I should have been extremely patient and used treats to lure her onto the dock. Frankly, she would have died of old age before she voluntarily placed one foot on the wooden planks. When she screamed, I told her "Quiet" (which she understood) and sat next to her, reassuring her with a positive tone. After a minute of that I picked her up again and put her down a few feet away. She only went halfway down but was still frozen on the spot. After a couple more times she understood that the dock wasn't going to "bite" her and she became okay with it.

Aside from being sensitive to a fault, Cheeta was probably the best-trained pharaoh hound in the country at the time. And I'm serious when I say that. Ask around and see if you can find anyone who knows of an off-leash trained sight hound. In the world of dogs, sight hounds have the best eyesight and are the fastest, with a strong predatory instinct. That's why greyhound adopters are told not to let the dog off leash. Scent hounds, bloodhounds, and beagles have the best noses. With Cheeta, I'm not talking about being off-leash in an obedience ring for ten minutes. I'm talking about telling her to wait outside a store in Manhattan while I went inside for something, or jogging through the streets of Queens, New York for three miles with her stopping at every curb without being told and not crossing the street until hearing me yell "Okay," even if I was a half a block ahead.

Have you ever met a sight-hound search dog? She sure had one of the critical requirements: perseverance. If I threw a rock into a pile of a thousand stones she would always search for the one with my scent on it, and never quit until she found it. I would have her sit and stay while I threw several stones or sticks into knee-high grass and tell her to "Bring." When there were multiple stones or sticks, I could see when she found one because her tail would wag furiously for a couple of seconds, but she wouldn't bring it to me right away. She would continue looking over other thrown items, but every once in a while she would check back, tail wagging, to make sure the already-found stick was still where she'd left it before continuing with her search. She was eleven years old when I first took her to several practice search-team training sessions at a local state park. She outdid two supposedly trained German shepherds when they quit from the heat. (Granted, Cheeta-Ann is a desert dog who thrives in heat, so probably she wouldn't have done as well had it been three degrees outside.)

The first time we took Cheeta to Jones Beach on Long Island, her desert heritage really presented itself. First, she started digging in the sand with her head swaying back and forth rhythmically as if in a trance while humming a really weird sound we had never heard before. It was something like a cross between mewling, howling, and growling. I remember Jaye saying "I think she lost her mind," while looking around furtively to see if anyone was watching, and then being totally startled by a cop approaching. Just as the cop arrived to give us a ticket for having an unleashed dog on the beach, Cheeta found a flat piece of wood, put her front feet on it, and started pushing and running, literally surfing across the sand with her front feet on the board. The cop, ticket book frozen in his hand, observed this for a few minutes, laughed, and said, "You have bigger problems than a citation for an off-leash dog on the beach!" He never gave us the ticket.

Despite her idiosyncrasies, Cheeta's gentleness with children was beyond extraordinary. She loved to play tug-of-war with a rubber ring. Whenever we had friends over, she would pick up the ring and put it into a guest's hand, enticing them to hold on. She was thin and only weighed about forty-five pounds, which was deceptive because if the guest was sitting on the couch and held on to the ring, he would find himself lying on his belly in the middle of the floor. However, when she offered the ring to two-year-old Tara or one of Tara's friends, she would gently shake it back and forth without the toddler having to let go or fall down. This wasn't something that was taught. Her gentleness with kids, the elderly, and the infirm was innate.

Coming home from the hospital with our first newborn, Tara, in Jaye's arms, I invited Cheeta-Ann to sniff Tara's feet, then the crown of her head. (Dogs should get lots of praise while introducing a new pack member.) I then gave Cheeta the positive association with Tara by giving her a very special treat, a hollow marrow bone stuffed with steak. She chose to hang out under the bassinet, staring at us the whole night with her beautiful expressive amber eyes, acknowledging the momentous change in our lives. It was a little eerie, like she was telling us we had to take this real seriously and be very conscientious. Every time Tara stirred or cried, Cheeta-Ann whined softly to tell us. As a matter of fact, Tara's first words were "Hi, Cheets." In the years that followed, two more two-legged members were added to the pack, daughter Kerry and son Brett. Thanks to my daughters, Cheeta-Ann had more clothing, jewelry, and sunglasses than most runway models. For more than fourteen years, Cheeta-Ann was a wonderful sister to them all.

Since Cheeta never showed a drop of aggression, I taught her a great trick. Pharaoh hounds smile a lot, and when a dog smiles it shows teeth. I taught her to smile on command using the command "Guard." I'd sit on the floor with Cheeta-Ann and a friend or two and put a pack of Marlboros on the floor between us. The guest would be told that the dog would guard anything I told her to. Then, I would tell the guest to reach for the cigarettes, but to do it slowly because I didn't want them to get bitten! As they slowly reached for the butts, Cheeta was told "guard" and immediately showed teeth. The closer they got to the smokes, the more teeth she showed, which caused everyone to withdraw. In truth, the only thing she ever bit was her food.

PART 6

COMING WHEN CALLED

I have to believe that virtually every dog owner would love to have their dog off-leash and perfectly responsive, but we can't program them to do what we want when we want; we can only condition them. But remember, a conditioned response is not a programmed response—it's not guaranteed.

Dogs, like people, have their own agenda. Not that they plan their activities weeks in advance—they basically live in the moment, following their agenda of the moment. Let's say your boxer Sweetbox is outside, off-leash, and twenty feet away and you call her to come. She knows what "come" means and usually cooperates. However, at this particular moment, a very handsome golden retriever happens to be walking by. Sweetbox is now faced with a dilemma. She wants to obey you, but she also wants to introduce herself to handsome Goldy, and her response may very well be, "In a moment, Mom, I *gotta* check out this potential boyfriend first." And you're left standing there wishing you had gotten a goldfish instead of a dog.

A dog refusing to come when called is much more likely to

take place outdoors off-leash than indoors off-leash, because a dog knows she's harder to catch outside. Starting your training indoors with success building on success is key. You will then move to a controlled outdoor environment and finally a large open space.

To begin, fifteen to twenty times a day, when your dog doesn't expect it, call her to come with a happy yet firm voice.

Step 1: Use her name first, then the command. "Sweetbox, come!" Do not keep repeating if the dog doesn't come. If your dog won't come the first couple of times you call her, walk past her with the treat in your hand, passing close to her nose, and call her.

Step 2: The split-second she starts to come, start praising her; it will keep her coming.

Step 3: Assuming your dog will sit on command, when she arrives, use a hand signal for the sit command. I would suggest your hand, palm up, going from your thigh to your chest as you say "sit." The moment her rear hits the floor, she gets a treat. A lot of people will use a down motion, but I like to go up. It will draw the dog's head up, which tends to bring her tush down.

The first four times you do this, she should always get a treat, and thereafter get the treat intermittently. That's the strongest way to condition an animal. Her attitude will become, "Maybe there's a treat, maybe not; I better go check it out." Also, as you practice, eliminate the spoken word "sit" and only use the hand signal so that she sits without being told and it becomes automatic.

If your dog is the type who looks at you, yawns, and doesn't move when you call her, start training using a dragging leash. Your dog needs to know that when you call her, it's not a suggestion, it's a command.

Step 1: Let your dog move around dragging a leash.

Step 2: Use her name first, then the command. "Sweetbox, come!"

Step 3: When you call her and she yawns and plays dumb, walk over, pick up the leash, and pull her to you with a smile on your face.

Step 4: Praise her lavishly when she arrives and give intermittent treats.

When your dog's indoor recall is excellent, it's time to take it outside, ideally in a small fenced yard. Now, you're going to turn things up and treat with people food. If the only time on planet Earth your dog gets people food is when she comes while off-leash outside, her off-leash recall will become much more reliable. Be it bologna or steak, find something that your dog loves. If she doesn't come, let her drag the leash, as previously mentioned.

Here's a great conditioner game that you can play with your dog:

Step 1: Call your dog and give her a treat immediately upon arrival.

Step 2: A family member who is a comfortable distance away should call her with people-food treats at the ready.

Step 3: The two of you can have the dog charging back and forth like a lunatic as she responds to the command "Come." Keep the words the same. It shouldn't be "Sweetbox, come" one time and "Here, puppy" the next.

Between the praise and the people-food treats, the three of you should have a blast as your dog flies back and forth between the two of you. Next, take it to the great outdoors. No fences.

Hopefully, you have a people-food treat so enticing that your dog hesitates leaving you. If she still does not come when called, let her drag a ten- to fifty-foot rope attached to a harness so that you can retain physical control. I recommend a fifty-foot light rope for a fast standard poodle and a ten-footer for a Chihuahua.

Practice these recalls a lot, and your dog will make you look like a dog whisperer! If progress is slower than you like, don't hesitate to call in a pro. The teaching methodology can vary greatly depending on your dog's personality, the size of your dog, the reaction to different distractions, and the intensity of the reaction. It's worth it.

PART 7

MANNERS

Manners matter. The well-mannered dog is a pleasure, while the ill-mannered dog produces stress and anxiety. I was standing in front of a couch when Louis the American bulldog was released from the bedroom. He barreled into me like a linebacker so that I ended up sitting on the couch with his sixty-five pounds on my lap as he farted and snorted fluids in my face to let me know how happy he was to see me. Physically trying to keep him out of my face as best I could, I shifted my head toward Sharon, his owner, and asked, "You don't get a lot of company, do you?" At which point she burst into tears. She hadn't been able to have a friend and Louis in the same room for months.

CHAPTER 25

HOW DO I GET MY DOG TO STOP STEALING FOOD?

I can't tell you how many times I've heard "That damn dog stole my dinner—again!" Or some variation of that. When you think about it, it's more instinct than stealing. We two-leggeds have about nine-thousand taste buds, and dogs only have about two thousand; that's why we've all seen dogs eat crap, literally. An animal in the wild will eat anything it can perceive as edible without hesitation and as quickly as possible, as opposed to us humans who make reservations at restaurants based on food we especially like, looking forward to savoring the meal.

If Klepto pretends he's not interested in the food on the coffee table when you're around, don't believe it. The moment you leave, it's fair game. Wanna stop Klepto from snatching your food? Introduce him to the Dog God. The Dog God sees all, all the time, and chastises dogs that pinch food off low coffee tables, kitchen counters, dining room tables, or anywhere else. And what is the Dog God's strategy for correcting a dog's thieving ways? Entrapment! Dogs primarily live in the moment, so timing is critical.

Step 1: Place a mirror so you can see where the trap will be sprung.

Step 2: Nuke a hot dog or fry a small piece of meat. Create that enticing meat smell!

Step 3: Take a small plastic container with a top and put a bunch of holes in it. Place the fragrant meat inside and close the lid. You definitely don't want Klepto to be able to self-reward by getting the meat. You want to entice him to reach for the meat and get no further than that.

Step 4: Put the container with the meat down, walk out of the room, and head over to the mirror. Klepto will think he's won the lottery when you leave the room.

Step 5: Make sure Klepto can't see you or associate you in any way with what is about to happen. This is crucial to your success. Have in your hand an empty soda can with twelve coins in it and a piece of Scotch tape over the opening so the coins don't fall out. If you don't have any cans handy, you can use any object or objects capable of producing a sound that surprises him when he's "stealing." An air horn, two pots banging, whatever works. Watch Klepto look around to make sure nobody is looking, then go for the gold. Just as his mouth reaches the container, send the soda flying into the room near him. Klepto will jump through the ceiling in surprise.

Remember, this has nothing to do with you, it's between Klepto and the Dog God. The shock is going to be related to *taking food off your table*. The Dog God sees all, all the time, and doesn't like it when you take anything off a table.

CHAPTER 26

HOW DO I STOP MY DOG FROM BEING TOO INTRUSIVE WITH GUESTS?

Many people usher their dogs to another room or part of the house when they are unruly or troublesome during parties or visits. It seems simple and straightforward, right? I wish I could tell you that locking your dog away is the solution, but it's not. It actually exacerbates the problem. At heart, dogs are social animals, so separating them from the group is like a "time out" for a kid. It's a punishment. Your dog just needs to learn manners.

For this situation, I suggest implementing the "Place" command. A "Place" command requires your dog to stay in the same spot until you release her. A leash attached to a floor molding or heavy piece of furniture should be hidden under the dog bed or place mat where Nudgy will hang out, ready to use if she strikes out. Make sure it's long enough for her to lie down on her bed, but no longer. Pick a spot for Nudgy in the loop of activity but out of the traffic pattern that enables her to see what's going on. When company arrives, bring Nudgy to the spot where she has been taught to lie down and stay. Always accompany the "Place" command with a special toy, be it a frozen Kong with peanut butter or a hollow marrow bone with a piece of meat or cheese wedged in the middle. If Nudgy leaves the place location to bother the guests, she should be calmly re-commanded to it. If she leaves a second time, she should be once again told "go to your place." Upon the third offense, she's struck out. Affix the leash, preventing her from being too intrusive with the guests. Have no pity. This command also comes in real handy for those guests who are afraid of or allergic to dogs.

However, keep in mind the "Place" command deals with your dog behaving civilly when your guests are already in the house. If Nudgy is ill-mannered at the door, there's no reason to expect that she will behave differently once the guests are inside. Usually the most difficult place to extract good manners is with the arrival of guests at the door. A solid door routine helps set a cooperative tone that is more likely to carry over into the rest of the visit. If Nudgy contains herself at the door, her response to the "Place" command should be much more reliable, making it less likely that she will be too intrusive. I strongly suggest that you take a look at Turmoil at the Door (pg. 75).

CHAPTER 27

WHY DOES MY DOG LICK EVERYTHING?

Dogs do a lot of licking. They explore the world primarily with their nose and mouth, so licking just feels good to dogs; it releases endorphins. If your dog could talk after giving you a good lick, she might say, "Your salty sweat is delicious, and it's obvious that you had red wine with your turkey sandwich, which, by the way, you neglected to share!" It was Mark Twain who said, "If dogs could talk, nobody would own them."

The problem is that dogs are strong creatures of habit, hence the constant, annoying licking of anything and everything. Your dog may be licking you to show affection or submission, or just enjoying the endorphins from your taste and close contact. When I'm on the floor breathing heavily doing push-ups, my dog Paula Jean licks the air in front of me, enjoying my extra-informative deep exhalations. Whenever I pet or cuddle Paula, she tries to lick me, and I just move and touch her in such a way that I avoid being licked. I call it the lollipop syndrome when I see someone sitting passively while their dog treats them like a Mad Martha ice cream cone. I remember a client trying to impress me with her close bond with her German shepherd by letting it lick her face for five minutes. The dog and I had just come in after a walk where the GS had licked all kinds of nasty stuff in the gutter, and then proceeded to lick his genitals in the elevator on the way up to her apartment. A simple handshake in lieu of a kiss would have sufficed.

It is also very possible that your response to your dog's licking you has inadvertently created positive reinforcement of the licking. Even if you say, "Cut it out!" she has learned that licking you will get some form of attention. More often than not, dogs will prefer negative attention to no attention. That being said, licking is not a problem to really worry about unless it is seriously obsessive, in which case the dog can give itself a "lick granuloma." The incessant licking of a sore spot, often on the front legs, can result in a lesion that keeps getting worse until it becomes a medical emergency. You can try to redirect this behavior with interesting toys such as a hard toy rubbed with a piece of baloney or cheese for a couple of seconds or any activity that will garner her interest more than licking herself will do.

There's one word I haven't mentioned so far that can create excessive licking: allergy. Your dog could be allergic to something in the environment or her food, which a vet can check for you. I suggest adding a daily dose of raw honey from local beekeepers (¼ teaspoon per twenty pounds of body weight). Raw honey has research-proven antibacterial and antimicrobial properties that can calm allergic reactions and soothe irritated skin.

CHAPTER 28

IS MOUTHING EVER OKAY?

Although mouthing is typical behavior for puppies, never let them get used to having teeth on you. Pups generally mouth a lot until they finish teething, which generally happens between four and six months of age, at which point the small, sharp teeth are replaced with much larger, less sharp ones. One of the ways to describe the maturation progress of dogs is to say that they go from puppy, to punk, to young adult, to adult, to adult-adult, to senior. I've seen young puppies run the gamut from being very sensitive to the displeasure of owners by displaying very little mouthing and jumping, to "the puppy from hell" that often acts like a four-legged shark, totally oblivious to their owner's negative reactions. The good news is that I've seen plenty of Jaws-like pups have complete turnarounds at about six months of age. It's almost like an epiphany; the dog hits that maturation point and starts cooperating because he realizes that he prefers your praise and treats to your sour face.

Until that time arrives, I suggest the following. Number one: exercise! As the old saying goes, "A tired dog is a well-behaved dog." Little Mouthy should be dragging a flat leash with the handle cut off so that you're better able to physically control him without your hands going to him negatively.

Number two: redirection. Redirect Little Mouthy's attention to a toy that is more attractive than your hands, pants, or chair leg. Try a hollow marrowbone with a piece of bologna in the middle so that he's very interested in the bone but can't quite get to the meat, or a tennis ball with a cut in it so you can put the bologna inside—that should keep him interested. There are also plenty of toys on the market that will garner his interest by having him work to get at the enclosed treat.

If your pup is in the punk stage and still mouthing, it has become a habit. Mouthy has to learn that teeth and flesh do not harmonize. Training a dog is letting the dog know that you either like the behavior or you don't *as the behavior is happening.* I don't use the word "No" when correcting a dog or pup because by the time I get there, many of the dogs think their name is "No Bad Dog." I say "uh-uh!" or "No teeth!" Let your pup drag a piece of leash (with the handle cut off and under supervision only), and when she starts to nip, grab the leash and apply a little pressure precisely when she's trying to nip. Then, substitute with a toy. If Mouthy's sitting on your lap and puts her teeth on your hand, don't pull your hand away; rather, with your other hand, twist her collar tight and give her a bit of discomfort as you snarl "No teeth!" The second she takes her teeth off your hand, release the collar and praise her lightly. Just make sure she feels a modicum of discomfort every time her teeth touch flesh, with the irritation stopping when she stops. Again, substitute with a toy.

DOG TRAINING DIARY

BRUNHILDA AND THE OPERA SINGER

"How many legs does a dog have if you call the tail a leg?
Answer: Four.
(Calling a tail a leg doesn't make it a leg.)"
—Abe Lincoln

I tell my kids (too often, they say), "The real luxury in life is not the yacht or Porsche or diamond, it's having a job you love to do." Mark Twain said it: "If you love what you do you'll never work a day in your life." I get paid to "play smart" with dogs. Nobody loves it more than I do. Nonetheless this particular work day was going to be a tough. I had four appointments scheduled, and they were all in Manhattan. The City injects its energy into everything, but it also takes a lot out, just by being there.

Four training appointments in one day is like being a comedian or actor and doing four shows a day. But these shows make no allowance for rehearsals or any kind of practice. They're all improv. When the front door opens, it's showtime! As I'm being introduced to the family and dog, I'm already at work. The first five seconds of my initial interaction with the dog are often critical. How easily can I get this dog to cooperate with its tail wagging? My body language, voice intonation, and eye contact vary immensely with each dog that I meet, always in response to the dog's behavior: frightened, bold, nervous, aggressive, shy. At the same time, I'm sizing up the owner, the environment, and the obvious problems. Putting on four shows a day takes a lot of energy.

What made this particular day tough wasn't just Manhattan; it was that all four appointments were first appointments, my first meeting with the dog. The day's first appointment wasn't till 1:30 p.m. The reason the lesson started after 1:00 p.m. was because Patricia, the dog's owner, is an opera singer and she doesn't get out of bed till the afternoon, at which time she has her brunch, which is served and cooked by her gourmet cook. The dog for whom I had been summoned was Brunhilda—Brunhilda the mastiff. She was one of three animals in the household. There was also Diva, the overweight Maltese, and Wigmor, the Persian cat. Brunhilda was a heavyweight. A sweetheart, but at 200 pounds she was definitely a heavyweight.

Brunch at Patricia's was an interesting spectacle. Bruny sat at Patricia's right elbow, her head higher than the table and therefore towering over it. Wigmor the cat was sitting *on* the table facing Patricia just off to the right at the two o'clock position. Diva sat on the floor at the left-front chair leg. Brunch at this household takes pretty long because Patricia only gets to eat every fourth bite. Each day a special plate of turkey is set out. The first bite goes to Bruny, the next to Wigmor, the third to Diva. Then Patricia gets to take a bite herself.

Dogs and cats being dogs and cats, this act of altruism on Patricia's part was not rewarded with a grateful, well-mannered thank-you on the part of her three furry diners. It. Was. Not. Bruny was downright invasive. Try putting a fork into your mouth while a massive furry head is nudging your hand and an eight-inch viscous river of drool is forming a little pool on the corner of the table. Wigmor was swatting at Bruny's head and the turkey dish while Diva was barking frantically, demanding her fair share.

Clearly my first appointment had been timed so I could witness this feeding fiasco, not just hear about it. This I much appreciated because I got to see the intensity of the unwanted behavior. The greater the intensity, the more difficult it is to turn it around. At this point I didn't know that Patricia was an opera star, but the elite Upper West Side address coupled with dark wood furniture so rich and vibrant that the elegant pieces reflected off each other like mirrors did indicate that she was comfortable.

At first, Patricia was trying to talk to me by ignoring the animals, who had returned to their customary positions after a very, very cursory examination of me. Conversation, however, was quite difficult with Patricia trying to talk over the furious barking while at the same time trying to protect her plate from Bruny and Wigmor. The more I said "What?" because I had missed half of what she said due to Diva's barking, the more frustrated Patricia became. Patricia is not accustomed to not being heard. Not with the melodic, resonant power of her voice. If you just met her on the street you'd be thinking, "Boy, with that voice she should be a singer."

Finally, pushing her chair back from the table she said vehemently, "This has to stop!" At which point her chief assistant and chef, Roland, stepped forward and said, "We have a prong collar and a head collar. How would you like to start?"

"Well," I said, while taking Wigmor off the table, "I'm going to put Wigmor and Diva in the bedroom with Valerie (an assistant who was folding laundry at the time) so that I can get Brunhilda's undivided attention. It will also make Diva a little jealous when she hears me praising Brunhilda, and that's okay." This isn't always so feasible because the separated dog might be the type to go nuts, diving at the door and screaming, but it was worth a try, especially because the bedroom was Diva's "den," the room where she sleeps, and she had the added comfort of Valerie's and Wigmor's presence. I placed Wigmor on the bed with the laundry and lured Diva into the room with a piece of turkey by slowly drawing it across her nose toward the bedroom and tossing it into the room when Diva was at the threshold. Smiling at Valerie, I said "Thanks," and closed the door.

Turning around, I collided with Brunhilda, who had followed her nose to my turkey-laden hand. Laughing, drawing the turkey past her nose, I said, "Not a chance, Bruny. You've entered the Shelby zone, land of 'nothin-fa-nothin.' You want a treat? Earn it." Human noses have less than half a square inch of olfactory tissue. Dogs average more than eleven square inches from their nose up to their eyes. When done correctly, walking past a dog's nose with a treat is powerful stuff. Brunhilda marched beautifully at my side back to the dining room.

"Talking the talk" is one thing, but the sooner you "walk the walk" the better. I always start working with the dog right away., and it's often so subtle that the owner isn't even aware that I'm testing and getting the dog to cooperate until they all of a sudden say, "Hey, how did you do that?" I love having the dog doing what I'm telling the owner I'm going to teach the dog to do all while I'm telling the owner I'm going to do it. (You got me?)

So, as Bruny and I entered the dining room, I turned and faced her, slowly ran my hand up past her nose, and said "Sit." When the head goes up following the treat, the butt comes down. When the butt hits the floor, the treat hits the mouth. Timing is critical. I then puffed my chest slightly as if I was a cop stopping traffic with a hand signal. "Stay," I said softly but firmly. I am now facing her full on, my body is not stiff, but it is confident, as is my eye contact—not threatening, but fully expecting cooperation. Brunhilda was not an egg-for-brain puppy. At age three, she was an adult who'd been around the block. She knew exactly what I wanted. She was thinking about testing me: her great size made her body language obvious. She intended to move to her left. I stepped a little toward her to my right, slightly invading her space while saying "Uh-uh!" Not loudly, but seriously. It stopped her dead in her tracks. I immediately backed off slightly, smiling and saying, "Thank you, good girl." I said this really sincerely because I *was* thankful—thankful that Bruny was a cooperative girl who was making me look good in front of Patricia and staff.

Still keeping half my body facing Brunhilda, I asked Patricia if she entertained a lot. Roland had already told me she loved to entertain and the dogs were way too intrusive: that's why I was called. "They practically ruined my last dinner party" was the terse reply.

"Well, Patricia, this is really fixable," I assured her. "I'm going to just teach them the basics and the basics include the door turmoil routine and a 'place' command." Patricia's raised eyebrows demanded further explanation. The "door turmoil routine," I explained, eliminates the turmoil at the door. "No more of Brunhilda's size and intrusiveness terrorizing your guests. No more out-of-control barking and crotch sniffing. Instead you will thank them for letting you know someone's at your door and then they will go to their respective spots, lie down, and wait till you verbally release them to politely say hello, if it's okay with the guest."

"Ha," was Patricia's response. "That'll be the day!" (I get that kind of response a lot when I explain the door routine.) I saw out of the corner of my eye that Bruny was getting restless so I stepped to her and slowly swept a small piece of turkey straight down to the floor past her nose as I said "Down." Her nose followed and she was delighted to be told (and cajoled) to lie down and get more comfortable.

Then, to Brunhilda, I said "Stay" and to Patricia I continued: "Not only will Bruny and Diva be well mannered at the door but when they're told to go to their place, they are going to go to a designated spot, lie down, and stay there." She laughed. "Now, for the bad news," I said. The laughter stopped on a dime. "Dogs are very, very habitual, and Bruny and Diva and even Wigmor will do what they gotta do to get their brunch-time fix! They've developed a 'habit' and, Patricia, you're the supplier. Feeding them from the table stops. That would be a good start."

The steely gaze I got in response was not very encouraging.

"Patricia, consistency is critical. You live with them. I only visit for an hour. I'll teach them what to do but you and your staff must create the new habits, the new patterns of behavior, and not undermine the progress by rewarding bad behaviors."

"In other words, you're saying I should end the highlight of their day" was more of a retort than a response from Patricia. I had a lady who wanted it both ways: the daily brunch parties *and* the well-mannered dogs. *Is it doable?* I asked myself. Sure, I could do it. I could bring them home, live with them for two weeks, and return them trained. But, without consistent follow-through, once they returned home Brunhilda and Diva would try to get away with whatever they could because that's what dogs do. Like most people, they get away with what they can. How far would they be able to push in this household? To tell the truth, because this was our first lesson, I didn't know. If Patricia was a serious taskmaster, the staff might be quite consistent.

Then I thought about how my wife, Jaye, would react to a 200-pound mastiff and a small dog that has "accidents" living with us for two weeks. Combined with Michelle and Mike, the two Dobermans in residence, we'd have over 400 pounds of dogs sharing our house with us. I have a very tolerant wife who agreed years ago to help board and train dogs, but Jaye has said to me several times over the years, "Why couldn't you have been a jeweler and brought that business home instead of these dogs?"

I backpedaled a little. "Okay, Patricia, you can have two well-mannered dogs whose training is undermined on a daily basis, but it will take a little longer and require real consistency from the whole household, especially from you. For starters, their meals from *your* table are going to be quiet and polite, a privilege that they will earn, not an entitlement. With their history, it's not going to be easy. As of today, like children, they need to understand and comply with *wait, quiet, leave it,* and *okay.*"

The rest of the lesson went quite smoothly, teaching the dogs beginning basics and getting Patricia and key staff members to imitate my body language, voice intonation, and timing. By the end, I was sitting at the dining room table and talking with Patricia and Roland with Brunhilda's head resting on my lap under the table. As I stood up from the table I could feel the front of my pants sticking to my thighs. In that instant I realized that the great warmth I had felt from Brunhilda's huge head was not just heat, it was *wet* heat. Brunhilda's drool had penetrated my underpants. Just as my eyes met Patricia's, all eyes in the room went to my crotch. I was mortified. *Turner & Hooch* flashed through my mind. What would Tom Hanks have said in this situation? What actually came out was a stammered "Brun–hil–da!"

Driving home after my last lesson that night, I thought of something Roland had told me that made me smile, and still makes me smile to this day. During one of the recent parties, when the apartment was filled with tuxedos and gowns, one of the well-endowed gowns had crouched down and snuggled Brunhilda a lot. When she stood up it looked as though she had entered and won a wet

T-shirt contest. "It was hilarious," said Roland, "but Patricia was not at all amused!"

It gave me an idea. I called from the car. "Did you forget something?" Patricia asked.

"First, I just want to say that you certainly did something very right, Patricia," I told her. "Both Brunhilda and Diva are very sweet." *And thank God for that*, I was thinking, *a 200-pound dog better be sweet*. "I had an idea I wanted to share with you. Why don't you consider getting aprons for your guests who interact with Brunhilda, so as to avoid the need for dry cleaning after they've schmoozed with her?"

The next time I saw Brunhilda, Roland asked me to put my arms straight out in front of me. He then slipped on a beautiful, full-length, down-to-my-knees canvas apron and tied it around my back. Across my chest was the name *Brunhilda* beautifully sewn in red script. "Miss Patricia loved the idea," he said with a smile. "And, boy, does it make things easier!"

Things got a lot better for a while until I got a call from Roland. "Patricia's in Europe on tour. She asked me to call you because things are out of control again."

"Is she back to the brunch routine with the dogs at the table?" I replied.

"What do you think?" was the answer.

That turned into a great lesson! I got paid my hourly rate to have a gourmet cook make me a delicious crab cake lunch (all crabmeat—no filler). I sent Bruny to her place, said one light "uh-uh" when she tried to leave the huge bean-bag chair that served as her place, and she was done. As for Diva, a couple of firm "uh-uhs" and she let out a large sigh of disgust and lay down next to Brunhilda. Wigmor I just swept off the table, and that was that.

The whole dog thing took about a minute and a half. Roland was a little upset that I was having such a peaceful lunch. "Shouldn't you be working with the dogs more?" he said petulantly. "Roland, I am training as we speak. By the way, this crab cake is the best I've ever had. How come? It's incredible!" That's when I learned about the no filler. "Roland," I explained. "The goal is to create a new pattern of behavior at the dinner table. Best way to do that is to have success build on success. As we speak I'm eating and the dogs aren't being intrusive at all. We're creating a new pattern of behavior. It's fantastic. As a matter of fact, I should have lunch here every day for the next two weeks until Patricia gets back. Show me a menu. They'll really be conditioned by then!"

I didn't quite get Roland's mumbled response.

Getting paid to eat a gourmet lunch was followed some time later by a request to meet them at the airport. Westchester Airport. At "the millionaire's hangar."

"Excuse me, the *what* hangar?" But I had heard her right: the millionaire's hangar. Patricia had a new jet and a new pilot and the on-ramp on this jet was narrower than the last one. Brunhilda was showing some aggression and Patricia wanted me to introduce Bruny to the new pilot and talk to him about handling her on the plane. She also wanted to get Bruny accustomed to the new ramp.

Another typical work day: waiting at a section of the airport I hadn't even known existed with a bunch of private jet owners. After a few minutes, an iridescent purple van arrived and Roland and Valerie hopped out. Inside were Brunhilda, Diva, and Wigmor. A minute later an iridescent purple Bentley arrived with Patricia in the back seat.

Patricia had me put Brunhilda in the back of the Bentley and the driver and I drove a few hundred yards to the new plane, pilot, and ramp. The plane was not as big as the jumbo jet I'd been imagining. On the way I said to the driver, "I didn't know Bentley made purple cars."

"They don't," he replied. "She had it custom painted."

"Great for resale," I said. He laughed at that. "What's a car like this cost?" I asked.

"About $200,000, not counting the paint job."

I had never been in a car that cost two hundred K before.

After I had Brunhilda follow a slab of meat up the ramp into the plane a few times, she loved the ramp, and the pilot. I took the rest of the day off after that lesson.

PART 8

PREVENTING PROBLEMS

Regardless of how many times I've said "It's a lot easier to prevent problems than to correct them," I've had my share of new dog owners saying to me, "I'm fine. I've had dogs before. I'll call you if I need any assistance." The desperate calls for help often came a few days later with tales of woe about the puppy's wanton destruction of shoes and antique furniture or he "doesn't understand a word I say," or "keeps peeing in the den out of spite!" A personal favorite of mine was Eddie Murphy's complaint about his dogs—"Why do they have to keep peeing on my ridiculously expensive white dining-room carpet?" Reaching out for some basic info to prevent problems with your dog is truly a lot easier than trying to fix them later on.

CHAPTER 29

HOW DO I STOP MY PUPPY FROM CHEWING ON MY STUFF?

About half of my training appointments have had to do with some kind of real behavioral issue, and destructive chewing is pretty high on the list. Many dogs have genuine preferences. I remember a redbone coonhound that just loved to spend an afternoon devouring a good book from the owner's library. There was the finicky wood eater—just chair legs for one particular Lab I got to know pretty well. More than once, the hapless owner went to sit down only to have the chair collapse as though the leg had been sawed through as a slapstick joke. Some of the wood eaters were strictly into door and floor moldings. The cloth eaters were killers. Imagine coming home to your four-piece sectional couch with three of the sections half shredded, along with the love seat. Carpets, yum! I don't think you can name a household item that a vet hasn't taken out of a dog's stomach. I know a golden retriever who was perfect in every way, except for the two operations he needed to remove his owner's stockings, which were completely tangled in his intestines. Let's not overlook the plastic-eating gourmets. Anybody not have any plastic in their house?

Why paper? Or wood? Or plastic? Dogs being creatures of habit, it very well could be happenstance. It was the first thing she got into and perhaps she liked the sound or feel of the crunch of the paper. Or maybe it was the taste or smell of the glue on an envelope. Another reason is attention. Many dogs prefer negative attention to no attention. Grabbing your favorite pair of shoes gets you to stop ignoring her, doesn't it?

I suggest not testing your dog's chew strength with supposedly chew-resistant toys or furniture. I've seen dogs break marrow bones and effortlessly demolish so-called indestructible dog toys. The "chew-proof" dog bed is just (maybe) going to take a little longer to destroy, but worse than that, it's going to reinforce a bed-chewing habit. To break a dog's destructive chewing habit, you will need to learn two things: the "Leave it" command, and redirection. Let's take a look at redirection first.

Puppies, virtually all of them, will chew on whatever they come across. Depending on the sensitivity of the dog, usually any startling noise when teeth are on something inappropriate will momentarily stop the chewing. This is when you jump in with redirection. Let's say you're sitting in front of the TV and see your puppy start to chew a chair leg. You bang the coffee table with your hand, a book, whatever, making sure the puppy doesn't see you doing it. This is important because you don't want the puppy to think it's okay to chew on a chair leg if you're not around or not looking. You need your pup to believe that it's the chair leg itself that doesn't like to be mouthed and produces the noise surprise. The noise shock will cause her to momentarily stop chewing the chair, at which point you instantly offer her and get her interested in an appropriate chew toy. *Redirection!* Your puppy gets startled when teeth are chewing anything inappropriate and immediately gets redirected to something appropriate. If she is cognizant of wanting to please you, saying "leave it" just before making the startling noise is okay.

Even if your dog learns not to chew wood (or anything else) in your presence, it's not good enough. She will need to be introduced to the Dog God, the god of dogs who sees all, all the time. And the Dog God doesn't like it when your dog chews on your stuff. Fill a can with a dozen pennies, placing it within easy reach, and hide. A whistle or blow horn can work, too. When you catch your pup chewing on your stuff, shake or throw the can to startle her. Whenever your dog's mouth touches your shoe, for example, you will startle her. Important: you can't be connected with the Dog God, so if need be, set up a mirror so she can't see you observing her.

The "Leave it" command is one that I recommend be taught to both dog and owner by a pro. In my opinion, a dog that does not understand and comply with the "Leave it" command is not a trained dog. In this chapter, we are looking at how it relates to puppies and chewing, but it is a fundamental command for dogs of all ages. The "it" in "Leave it" can apply to anything. When walking your dog on leash you may want him to ignore another animal or food on the ground. The "Leave it" command is even more important if your dog is off leash because you lack physical control. The properly trained "Leave it" command saves dog lives.

The International Association of Animal Behavior Consultants proposed the LIMA (Least Intrusive, Minimally Invasive) concept, which has always been my training philosophy, as opposed to "All Rewards Training." I'm a "depends" trainer. One size never fits all! Depending on the sensitivity and responsiveness of each dog, and the intensity of the need for "Leave it," the training method I use *depends*.

What I've done in thousands of households is have the dog owners place a plate with meat on it on the floor in the middle of a room while the dog and I are in another room. I walk in with the dog on his leash. Inevitably, the dog heads straight for the plate of meat. Just before he gets to it, I say "Leave it," immediately followed by a leash snap. The leash snap is a very quick jerk on the leash to the side, avoiding impact and pressure on the trachea. The leash must be loose! *There should be absolutely no restraining or pulling on the leash.* It's best if there are a couple of metal tags on the collar because the chinking sound of the tags will add to the dog's surprise. When timed right, Bowser will relate the negativity of the surprise to avoiding whatever he's focused on when he hears "Leave it." As soon as he leaves it, he should get treats and praise. In most cases, literally thousands of times in my training experience, this correction works. Bowser is loving the praise and treats for ignoring the "nasty" plate of meat on the floor after two or three corrections (leash snaps) as we walk by the plate with a loose leash.

If these strategies are not yielding the results that you want or need, you may want to consider using an electric shock or e-collar. A good e-collar will enable you to use tone (sound), collar vibration, and stim (electric shock), which can be effective *if used properly*. Even if your dog is 150 yards away, the e-collar allows you to get his attention. Learning is best done with the guidance of a pro. Do not figure it out on your own, especially if you are dealing with predatory aggression. When I recommend the use of an e-collar, I am always present to instruct the owner in its proper usage. *Always.* I'm a "depends" trainer. The intensity of the need for "Leave it" depends on the sensitivity and responsiveness of the dog.

To begin, I tell dog owners to put the e-collar on the dog without activating it, read the instruction manual, and leave the remote in the box until I get there. By the time I arrive, Stubborn Scottish Terrier will have forgotten about the new collar on his neck. This is to avoid him getting "collar wise," thinking he only has to behave when the collar is on. I then do the lesson with the e-collar making sure the dog owner understands how to use the e-collar properly.

Like the plate with meat on the floor, I tell owners to be prepared with several things planted to tempt their dog so they can practice the "Leave it" command. It can be a tennis ball rubbed with a piece of cheese, whatever. If Stubborn Scotty, wearing the activated e-collar, comes across the cheesy tennis ball and leaps two feet in the air when I call out "Leave it," there's no need for vibe or stim. If the reaction to the tone is a yawn, I go to vibe. If that too elicits a yawn, I continue on to stim. Some e-collars have a stim intensity that goes from one to one hundred. I have never, ever, used stim on a dog without stimming my own hand first. On a one to one hundred e-collar, I've often felt close to nothing at seven or ten. I need to know what the dog will be feeling and judge what is appropriate, again, depending. For a large aggressive dog with the sensitivity of a rhino, I'll use a stronger stim than I would for a Chihuahua.

You may notice that many of the e-collar instruction booklets suggest that you start with a very low stim and raise it as is necessary. I *absolutely disagree*. In my experience, doing it that way— starting low and raising the stim level because the dog adapted to the lower level—is self-defeating. The last thing I want is for the corrections to get harsher and harsher. I start at a level that shuts down the unwanted behavior immediately and enables me to consistently bring the stim level down because Stubborn Scotty becomes very sensitive to the command "Leave it." It also enables me to replace stim with tone or vibe. If the command "Leave it," is instantly followed by tone, then stim, very quickly you may find that you don't need stim at all. Stubborn Scotty will cooperate on the "Leave it" tone to avoid the stim. Soon you will only need to say "Leave it," which is the ultimate goal.

CHAPTER 30

HOW DO I GET MY DOG TO UNDERSTAND MY INSTRUCTIONS?

I have three kids who were all taught right from wrong. Does that mean they always did right? Absolutely not! Countless times I've said to my clients, "I have good news and I have bad news. The good news is your dog is real smart, and the bad news is your dog is real smart—and not cooperative." Dogs are not computers that we can program. Your dog may be off-leash looking at the cute Jack Russell walking by when you call her to come, and she knows what "come" means, but she makes a decision: "In a minute, Mom! Just gotta check out this Jack!" Dogs will play stupid and be manipulative to get away with what they can just as often as people, especially when they're young. The first step in getting your dog to cooperate is to make your instructions clearly understood.

Many dog owners make the common mistake of using too many words when trying to communicate instructions to their dog and speaking with increasing volume as each attempt fails. I once did a training seminar in an auditorium and had a student sit in a chair on stage as I leisurely walked around him while speaking nonsensical double-talk. I asked "Wo erA u-oy yay-dott?" In other words, "How are you today?" When I asked him if he knew what I was saying, he said he didn't understand one word, and was I speaking Greek? "That's what your dog understands when you speak in sentences," I said. "Nothing! Later on, your dog may pick out a key word in a sentence, but when giving training commands it's important to keep then as simple as possible." As for shouting, I'm reminded of when I was in Italy and asked someone for directions, hoping he spoke some English as I speak no Italian. Well, he spoke no English, and when he tried telling me where I needed to go, he got louder and louder until he was practically screaming at me because of my lack of comprehension. Needless to say, if you don't understand the words, making them louder doesn't help. You also need to recognize that your dog's hearing is far superior to your own. When I was on a high-priority search with my dog, meaning that the missing person I was looking for was very possibly still alive, I used to call out the person's name and blow a whistle, and then observe my dog. If she cocked her ears and looked in a specific location, perhaps the missing person had responded below my hearing ability, but not hers. Just as the teacher in a classroom is talking as opposed to yelling, you shouldn't shout to get your dog to cooperate. I know of a border collie who has a verified vocabulary of more than a thousand words, more than any other dog out there to my knowledge. That vocabulary was built up over many years with careful and precise schooling. I can say to my dog Paula Jean, "I'd like to go to dinner and the movies and a party, so would you be so kind as to *hurry* up and relieve yourself before I'm gone for hours?" And she'll get it. But she's a well-trained adult dog.

It is best to use single word commands, especially when you are starting to build your dog's vocabulary. Understanding and cooperation starts with single-word commands precisely timed with the action it represents. Let's go through a basic and essential command, telling your dog to go outside to relieve himself. A good one-word command for this is "Out." Emphasize the word "out" just before you open the door that takes him to the relief area, and he will soon recognize the word "out" and what it represents. When it comes to educating your dog, timing is everything. As soon as he finishes peeing or pooping, and only then, reward him with praise and a treat. Do it immediately (not when you get back in the house) so that you are clearly connecting the desired action and the reward. Remember, good training is letting your dog know you like or don't like the behavior *as it is happening*. If you're happy when your puppy peed outside but don't give him a treat until he gets inside and sits next to the treat cabinet, the dog will associate the treat with coming in the house, not peeing outside.

Along with timing, consistency with the command words is critical. If you want your dog to come and you say "Bowser, come" but your wife says "Here, puppy, puppy" and your son says "Hey, Bowser, over here" your pup will be confused and take much longer to understand what you would like him to do. Pick one command that everyone agrees on and stick to it.

CHAPTER 31

WE'RE MOVING. HOW DO WE HELP OUR DOG ACCLIMATE TO HIS NEW ENVIRONMENT?

Countless times I've heard, "My dog's behavior is regressing; she started destructive chewing again like when she was a puppy, or peeing in the house," or whatever, for no reason at all. But there's always a reason, and it's my job to find out what's causing the dog's aberrant behavior. Dogs are very aware and sensitive to the vibe of the household. The sadness of a wife whose husband passes away may create enough anxiety in the family dog to cause it to start nervously chewing on furniture again.

If you're moving because of a catastrophic change in your life, your dog is likely to be depressed or a basket case before the move even occurs. Add to that the fact that your dog can't even conceive of the concept of "moving," what the dog will perceive is the disassembling of her den, her sanctuary, with no understanding of "why."

When my wife Jaye and I decided to move to Martha's Vineyard to retire, it was all for the good, yet Jaye cried for most of the five-hour drive from New York just because of the trauma of the momentous change in our lives. So, even assuming that your move is positive, all your dog may see is your stress from the actual mundane hassles of moving all your stuff.

So, what to do? If possible, before you move, bring your dog to the new house. Make sure he's hungry and feed him there. Play with him there. Walk him in his new neighborhood. Do this as often as you can. If you can't actually get into the house, familiarize him with the area around the house as much as possible. And when you do move, make sure that his bed and bowl and toys are in the new digs immediately, not in a storage facility to be picked up later. If possible, endeavor to stick to your dog's familiar routines to which he is accustomed: feeding, walking, playing times, etc. There's comfort in knowing the routine. Stay upbeat and try to make it a fun new adventure as if you were taking your dog for a hike to a new area.

PART 9

YOU KNOW YOU WANT TO ASK

I've found that a lot of dog owners, especially new ones, are embarrassed by some of their dog's behaviors, not knowing that these seemingly demented or ludicrous exhibitions are normal or not uncommon for our K-9 brethren. As my wife Jaye likes to say, "That's the dog in them!" And she's absolutely right.

CHAPTER 32

WHY IS MY DOG RUNNING AROUND THE HOUSE LIKE A LUNATIC?

I've had quite a few frantic calls over the years in which the panicked dog owner exclaims that their dog "has gone berserk," "lost his mind," or "is trying to kill himself!" In response to one such call, I inquired about the "suicidal" puppy. I was told that the puppy in question was zooming around the apartment at top speed, and was smashing into the same wall, skidding on the wood floor, trying to make a turn. Those times when a dog gets excited and doesn't calm down easily are often referred to as FRAP (frenetic random activity periods). Simply put, they're energy releases, more often than not joyous, and all healthy dogs have them.

A good way to calm this behavior is redirection. When Hyper starts to act crazy, let him know you have a treat, and practice "sit," "stay," and "go find." Tell him to sit and stay, and then throw a treat while still enforcing the stay command (step on the leash if you have to). Then, tell him to "go find the treat" and let him go. Make the treat increasingly harder to find with each throw. He'll love the game!

A walk in the rain will often induce a dog to temporary insanity because a natural way of getting dry and warm is jumping and running around like a nut. If you have access to a backyard, enter with Hyper on a leash. This will allow you to have much control if his FRAP kicks in and he starts getting obnoxious, slamming into you, and mouthing. Better yet, before he has a chance to go into his play mode with the wild eyes that say, "I'm going to play-attack you and it's all in fun," redirect his attention to earning your praise and treats for his cooperation, just like the indoor treat scenario. Tell Hyper to "sit," and when he does, give him a treat. Work him for a minute with a couple of "sits" and "stays," and then throw a treat for him to find and devour. A great exercise is getting Hyper to sit and stay when you throw a treat, and instead of immediately going after the treat, have him hold the stay until you say "Okay," releasing him to find the treat.

Some dog owners have asked me if they should use a crate to calm their dog. You can do this, but you need to make sure it isn't perceived as punishment. Use treats to get Hyper to sit, and then introduce whatever word you want to get him into the crate and toss a treat in. Once Hyper follows the treat in, close the door and toss a few more treats into the crate.

CHAPTER 33

WHY IS MY DOG EATING POOP?

The habit of eating poop is called coprophagia, and it's not terribly uncommon, especially the eating of other species' feces. Most dog owners on Martha's Vineyard have seen their dogs occasionally nibbling on goose poop. It's a little less common for them to eat their own species' feces, but as my wife says when dogs do disgusting things, "It's the dog in them!" The worst case I encountered was a Shih Tzu that turned around while defecating and gobbled up the feces as soon as it hit the floor. It was ironic, because the "Shit" Tzu's owner produced TV ads for breath mints.

Training a dog is based on timing. Dogs basically live in the moment, so as the behavior is happening, they need to know that the behavior is acceptable or not. There is a solution I've employed many times for the coprophagic dog, with total success. The interaction has to be strictly between the dog and the poop. From the dog's perspective, the human has nothing to do with it. It's poop versus dog. Period. If you correct DD (Disgusting Dog) when you see him eating feces, he will only learn that he can't do it when you're looking. I've found the best solution to be an electric shock or e-collar. Please be advised, though, I never suggest that someone use an e-collar on their dog without first working with a trainer. The decision of whether to use tone, vibration, or stim, and the intensity of the stim, should be made by an experienced professional as it depends on many factors such as the dog's temperament, size, and sensitivity as well as the behavior that needs to be modified.

The first thing to do is put the collar on DD and leave it on him for a couple of days so he forgets about this new thing on his neck. You don't want him to become "collar wise." In other words, he believes that he only has to behave when the collar is on. Keep the remote in your pocket or clipped to your belt. When DD goes to pick up the poop, he gets a tone, or vibration, or mild electric stim, depending on his sensitivity. Act as though you had nothing to do with it. If DD experiences something unpleasant every time he picks up a turd, the behavior will be extinguished quickly (unless he's a masochist). You want DD to relate the negative surprise, be it tone, vibration, or stim, to the poop-grabbing, not you. In my experience, if timed correctly, it won't take more than a few applications of negative surprise for the message to be received by the dog. I had a case at a dog run in NYC with a very well-trained Lab that was a feces glutton, zooming around the dog run snacking as fast as she could. She was about as sensitive as a tank, so I used electric stim, and the result was comical. When we let her loose, she immediately grabbed a turd, which flew out of her mouth as soon as I stimmed her. She then circled the turd, growling at it. Perfect! The bad guy was the turd, not us. The owner told me the nasty habit was totally eradicated in three days with a total of about five stims.

There are several theories as to why dogs eat poop, from trying to compensate for a nutritional deficiency to trying to hide the poop because the owner always gets angry when he finds it. Regardless of the many theories as to why they do it, eating fecal matter isn't just a nasty habit; it's also a potential health hazard for your dog.

CHAPTER 34

WHY DOES MY DOG PEE FROM EXCITEMENT?

Take heart. Pretty soon your friends won't have to wear rain pants and waterproof shoes to come for a visit. You'll be greeting them with wine instead of paper towels and vinegar. What you're dealing with is called nervous wetting. Lots of people call it happy pee, although no one is happy about it. Believe it or not, in the canine world, peeing is a polite way for a dog to greet what he considers a higher authority, and for the "soft" dog, it's the way of an ingratiating, friendly hello.

The more emotional the visitor is, the more emotional the nervous wetting response (and the more to clean). You know the type, the guest who enters and gushes all over the dog. The worst thing you can do in that moment is chastise the dog because he'll just pee more trying to appease your obvious displeasure. The first order of business is warning friends and family to enter your house without acknowledging Friendly Fido, basically ignoring him. At most, a split second of fleeting eye contact with Fido coupled with a half second "Hi, Fido" and smile. That's it. As the emotion at the door decreases, so will Fido's reaction. This solution is also incorporated into what I call the door routine, designed to eliminate the turmoil of aggression: jumping, barking, or whatever unwanted behavior your dog presents at the door. You can read all about that in Part 4.

CHAPTER 35

HOW DO I CALM MY DOG DOWN DURING THUNDERSTORMS?

Lots of dogs are fearful during thunderstorms. My search and rescue Doberman Michelle was afraid of nothing until age thirteen. Then, out of nowhere, I saw her cowering in fear at a booming thunderstorm. I responded by redirecting her attention. I started playing wildly with her, rolling on the floor with her, being silly, or conning her into engaging in play with me. I quickly gave her a treat when she went into a half-a-play bow, or even smiled at my antics. I worked hard at giving her something else to think about, something fun and happy to engage in.

Your first line of defense, as the thunder is rolling, is to play very vigorously at the first sign of anxiety. If your dog is having a great time during the thunderstorm, you're on the road to desensitizing the dog to the noise. To fully desensitize your dog to the sound of thunder, play recordings of thunder. Have your dog hang out in a favorite spot and play the sounds softly enough that he barely hears them as you give him tiny pieces of steak. Then, with success building on success, patiently raise the volume of the fake thunder. Your dog might be able to handle these sounds better if they are associated with steak.

In addition to sound, there is another element to thunderstorms that can be upsetting to dogs—barometric pressure changes—which often result in static electric shocks. If I touch a sweater and get a mild static shock, I know that it's no big deal, but the dog who gets a static shock when his nose touches the couch or your finger doesn't understand and can easily get anxious. I recommend a Storm Defender Cape used in combination with a ThunderShirt or anxiety wrap for dogs that continue to get freaked out by static shocks and thunderstorms. Storm Defender Capes are effective in eliminating static-electricity shocks. ThunderShirts or anxiety wraps, when cinched tightly around the dog, helps ground the dog and often reduces anxiety levels. I've seen lots of dogs helped by all of the above. What you want to show your dog is that life goes on *as usual*, even during a thunderstorm.

CHAPTER 36

HOW DO I KNOW WHEN IT'S THE RIGHT TIME TO PUT MY DOG TO SLEEP?

My heart goes out to all dog owners who have to deal with the terrible decision to euthanize their dog and its remorse-filled aftermath. How do I tell a family to kill their dog? Over the years, I've given the "when and how to say good-bye" a lot of thought, be it for disease, injury, or behavior.

I don't think anybody loved his work more than I did as a dog trainer, yet I had several incredibly dire, dreadful days every year. Of my more than 800 training appointments per year, about half were for problem dogs, and aggression was usually the biggest problem. I've met my share of seriously dangerous dogs, resulting in my needing to tell two to four families per year that their dog needed to be euthanized. Even knowing in my heart that it was the right decision, it was still agonizing.

For the sick dog, the "when" is a total judgment call based on your observations. If Pardner is either crying in pain or unconscious from painkillers, the decision is a little easier. It's when he's "hangin' in," still getting some enjoyment from life, that the "when" can be really difficult. Really hard. When my beloved pharaoh hound Cheeta-Ann stopped eating dog food, I went to steak, chicken, and eggs, but when she stopped drinking, I did what I had to do. You have to observe Pardner's discomfort, and when your heart tells you it's time, don't kid yourself, *do it*.

As for the "how," make it as painless for Pardner as possible. If the vet can come to you, great. The vet can give him a pill to get him nice and relaxed. If Pardner's amenable, perhaps you can offer a delicious piece of food to joyfully munch on as he gets the shot. My beautiful Cavalier King Charles spaniel Tri Guy died with his tail wagging furiously as he ate a chocolate bar.

Whether the capacity for your dog to enjoy life is totally diminished due to old age or illness, and that fateful decision needs to be implemented, I suggest that you not share your depression with him, adding to his discomfort. Bear in mind that there's no domestic animal that reads the body language and voice intonation of humans better than dogs. He reads your voice, your eyes, your whole body. If you're sobbing and wailing while hugging your ailing dog, it's not going to make him feel better. On the contrary, it's going to scare and depress him further. Instead, love him with happy hugs, pointing out the beauty of being alive, enjoying the sunny day, brisk breeze, or whatever. When it's over, you can mourn till you can't mourn anymore. Tri had been diagnosed with cancer of the tonsils, and when it was time to let go, my wife Jaye and I were upbeat and positive as he got the shot. Then we mourned and cried till there were no more tears left. Mourn afterward, not before.

CHAPTER 37

WHY IS MY DOG ROLLING AROUND IN DISGUSTING STUFF?

Dogs often do disgusting things—at least from our human perspective. I adopted my poodle Paula Jean at age two. After a million off-leash walks with her all over Martha's Vineyard, one day she decided to roll in some very nasty looking and smelling diarrhea. Years ago, my pharaoh hound rolled in a can of rotting tuna fish and sliced her neck on the broken can, requiring stitches.

Dogs explore the world primarily with their nose and mouth, so to dogs, a scent is generally not a matter of good or bad; it's a matter of the stronger the better. The stronger the smell, the more informative it is. I don't have enough fingers to count all the times I arrived for a lesson and, to the embarrassment of the owner, the puppy came bounding into the room with a tampon or underwear in its mouth. That's why they like to chew on shoes, preferably the ones you just took off after jogging. When you come home and your dog smells your pants, it knows who you touched, what you ate, and what environment you were in.

A hunting wolf will roll in a decomposing animal carcass to

disguise its scent in order to get closer to its prey, so when a domestic dog rolls in the unmentionable, I believe it's a piece of instinct inherited from its wolf ancestors, even though they're not hunting for anything. To our chagrin, the clueless dog smells it, and just feels as though it's the right thing to do at the moment.

I don't think this is a preventable behavior through training. Instinct being instinct, the best you can do is read the body language before it happens and with an "uh-uh" (for the well-trained dog) stop the roll as it's starting. The roll invariably starts with the dog bending down and turning his head sideways, looking to start the roll on the side of his neck. Prevention, of course, requires the owner to be lucky enough to see the off-leash dog present the aforementioned body language.

DOG TRAINING DIARY

A VIEW FROM THE TOP, DELAYED
BY A RABID RACCOON

"My dog is half pit bull, half poodle.
Not much of a watchdog—but a vicious gossip."
—Craig Shoemaker

The call came from Penelope, the new client's assistant, and I knew by the way she said the name that the dog owner wasn't a guy with the same name, he was *the guy*, the tantrum throwing tennis player. I get lots of calls from assistants, major domos, personal secretaries, and the occasional chauffeur-bodyguard. Most RAFs (Rich and Famous) don't make their own dog training appointments. Tantrum Thrower is an RAF. His Rockstar wife is also a RAF. They wanted to see me right away—tomorrow. Great. I rearranged a couple of appointments so I could see them first, when I was most fresh.

Even though I've probably been in the homes of a hundred RAFs, it's still exciting. I'm always psyched to meet them and see how they live. I want to be at my best, make a good impression, especially the first visit, so why is it that unexpected *stuff* always seems to happen before an RAF appointment?

At the time, my family was living across the street from a state park. Our house sat on over an acre of land, and I had fenced in an area off the mudroom, about seventy by forty feet, so I could let the dogs out to relieve themselves without having to walk them. The night before my first meeting with my new RAFs, I let my dogs Mikey and MacDuff out for their last bathroom break before bed. The mudroom was all windows. As I approached the door to let the dogs in, MacDuff was barking and I saw Mike streaking across the lawn. Having experienced Mike's predatory aggression too many times over the years, I quickly threw open the door and yelled "Leave it!" Too late. Whatever it was, it was pretty large and it was hanging limp in his mouth.

Great. I grabbed a garbage bag and a pair of gloves and approached Mike with his dead prize. He was standing there, head held high, ears erect, proud as could be with his kill. I told him, "Drop it!" After I repeated the command a second time, he did, reluctantly. MacDuff was barking the whole time, very excited by the whole scene and probably trying to take credit for the kill. I picked up what turned out to be a large adult opossum and placed it in the garbage bag, which I then put in a garbage can. Luckily the next day was garbage pickup. I was thoroughly disgusted with the unnecessary slaughter of a four-legged nocturnal neighbor, but that was Mike. Fortunately, when he was working, when he had his vest on and was looking for missing people, he was more enthusiastic and focused on the search, and he paid little interest to the animals we encountered.

Predatory aggression varies from dog to dog and is often confused with a herding response. The dog that chases the jogger, skateboarder, or moving car might be trying to herd it—or he might be trying to kill it. Movement elicits a prey response in almost all dogs. That's why the puppy chases the blowing leaf and why the last thing you should do if you meet an aggressive dog is run. If the puppy nipping at your kid's heels is a Shetland sheepdog, it's most likely trying to herd the child.

The next morning, I took the household garbage out to put in the cans for pickup. When I lifted the cover off the can, the not-so-dead opossum leapt up at me. I screamed and almost fainted. Ever hear the expression "Playing possum?" Now we know where that came from! This guy had both Mike and me convinced that he was dead.

After my adrenaline rush, I dragged the can to the twenty-eight-acre field adjacent to my property and tipped it gently over with a little prayer—"Hope your injuries aren't too bad and you live a happy life"—as the opossum exited the can and slowly disappeared into the brush.

Almost every day started with an hour or so walk up the state park mountain across the street from my house. Today I was especially looking forward to it because it was a beautiful autumn morning, colors galore, and I wanted to give some thought to the opossum experience and clear my head before my appointment with the RAFs. The entrance to the park was about 150 yards down the road with a huge beautiful wooden gate that required my whole body leaning into it to open it. The moment I was inside, I'd unhitch the dogs from their leads and they'd usually charge up the mountain with unbridled joy. About a quarter of a mile into the walk I heard a serious commotion. Shit! This time it was a very large raccoon, and he was definitely not playing dead. I heard myself screaming, "Not again, Mikey!"

I had to assume that the raccoon was insane with rabies because raccoons are nocturnal and this one was out in broad daylight. He was huge, and he was fighting Mikey ferociously for his life. MacDuff was darting in and out for quick bites while barking like a lunatic. My behavior was probably similar to Duff's except I wasn't trying to bite, just darting around yelling "Leave it!" while looking for a suitable stick to try to separate Mike and the raccoon and protect ourselves. Finally, Mike got a death grip, shook the poor animal, and dropped it at last after I'd screamed "Drop it!" multiple times while shooing a very excited Duff away with the stick. So much for clearing my head with a beautiful autumn walk.

Mike's face was covered in foam, spittle, and blood, and to my dismay, though unconscious, the raccoon was still breathing. Without touching either dog (contact with the saliva or blood of a rabies-infected animal with any kind of open wound can transfer the deadly infection), I leashed them both and hurried back to the house. I then donned latex gloves and cleaned Mikey off, looking for wounds. There was a three-inch-long scratch on the side of his head below the ear, probably a claw mark from the raccoon's sharp nails, but I found no bite punctures. MacDuff was unscathed. Then, I grabbed my new police "off-duty" pistol and went back up the mountain to put the raccoon out of its misery.

On the way to my mercy killing, I called my vet to tell him that both Mike and MacDuff needed rabies boosters. Not until I got back to the house did I realize that I should have brought the raccoon's body off the mountain to be checked by the health department to confirm rabies. At this point, I had used up the time I would have taken had it been a normal morning mountain walk, and I did not want to be late for my RAF appointment, so I then made the mistake of saying to my wife, "Honey, I don't want to be late for my first lesson with *the* Tantrum Thrower, so please do me the favor of bringing the dead raccoon back from the mountain so the health department can check it for rabies. Take gloves and a strong plastic bag because it's heavy and covered in blood and spit." As I said all this, Jaye's normally friendly face was contorted with fury as she lashed out at me and stormed out of the kitchen. It dawned on me at that moment that a frontier wife of the 1800s might do that if asked, but an upper-middle-class suburban speech pathologist might find the request, shall we say, unreasonable.

Later that night we were out for dinner with another couple, Hank and Lynn, and Jaye told the story of what I had asked her to do. My good friend Hank initially thought she was joking and Lynn stared at me, slowly shaking her head and wagging her finger at me as though I was crazy. As a matter of fact, every friend we have has heard the story from Jaye and the best I got from some of the guys was congratulations for having the guts to ask such a favor.

Needless to say, I trudged back up the mountain to retrieve the corpse, only to have the health department tell me when I called that "we don't need to see it, we know there's rabies about!" So, I still had to call the RAFs and tell them I'd be a little late. The thought did cross my mind to shock the trash collector by leaving the dead raccoon on top of the garbage and filming the guy's reaction when he lifted the cover. But Jaye, still in a snit about my telling her to get the dead raccoon, definitively killed that idea.

The address was pure RAF: Central Park West across the street from the Museum of Natural History. For what it's worth, I once got to ride down in the elevator with Seinfeld in this building. Tantrum Thrower is a world-famous athlete who married a well-known entertainer after divorcing an Oscar winner. This was another one of those trainings where the reason for my being there, the dog, was the least interesting thing about the lesson. Lulu, the five-month-old poodle mix, was a cute, normal puppy that just needed some proper direction.

The apartment, however, was outrageous, starting with the lobby of the building. Not that it was fancy or opulent; it was austere, almost cave-like, with subdued lighting and twists and turns, nothing like the usual lobby you see with the two couches, bureau, flower pot, and mirror. In my own house we seriously redecorated after Brett, the youngest child, was mature enough not to wreck everything and to take pride in his surroundings. It seemed similar here. Between the ex-wife and his present wife, there were several pre-teen kids, but I never got a handle on who was who because they were constantly coming and going. I did, however, enjoy their presence as they were all sharp and inquisitive about the dog training, not to mention incredibly athletic (we know where that came from), basically cartwheeling around the apartment. I figured the redecorating would happen when the cartwheeling slowed down. What made the apartment outrageous was its third floor. It was a triplex! Kind of rare in NYC apartment buildings.

I never got to meet Mr. Tantrum Thrower himself. He was out of town, so all my interaction was with his wife, and although I got the vibe that she didn't like me a whole lot, the kids and Lulu did, so it was okay. When I mentioned—in front of the kids, of course—that Lulu was a good candidate for some cool tricks, their cries for tricks overrode Mom's objections. So, to the great enjoyment of the kids, and even a few smiles from her, Lulu learned to roll over and drop dead when shot by a hand in the shape of a gun while they said "Bang."

The fun stuff was taught after Lulu was trained to go to a particular spot, lie down, and stay—what I call a "Place" command. As I tell people, "When the dog is told to go to place, it has to stay there for six months, or whenever you release her, whichever comes first." Lulu being a young puppy, all this stuff was taught in a little over two and a half hours. At the end of the lesson, I looked at my watch and said, "The lesson took over two and a half hours, but I'm only going to charge you for an hour and a half because it was so much fun with the kids." The Rockstar wife responded with hostility: "You must be the most expensive dog trainer in the world!" I might have exacerbated her anger when I answered, "I hope so."

Anyhow, one of the best parts of this job was Penelope. She was like a co-conspirator. At one of the lessons the Rockstar wife said, "Back in a while, have to run some errands."

Penelope appeared a few moments after the door closed. "Want to see the tower room? It's really cool!"

"What about Mom?" I asked.

Penelope shrugged. "I know where she's going. She won't be back for a couple of hours. Wait a minute, I'll make sure she left the building." Then she called down to one of the doormen: "Has Mrs. Rockstar left yet?"

"Just missed her, but I could probably catch her" came the doorman's reply.

"No, no, it's okay, it's nothing important," said Penelope, clicking off the intercom. Smiling, she urged me to follow as she headed for the stairs. "Check this out. I love this place. It's really outrageous," she said as she pounded up the stairs with me in hot pursuit.

"What about Francis?" I asked as we passed the kids' bedrooms heading for the stairs to the tower room. Francis was another assistant who was also always there whenever I came.

"If she hears us she'll probably join us" was Penelope's giggly reply. I pride myself on my professionalism and don't normally fool around like this, but I'll admit I got caught up in the moment and thoroughly enjoyed the sneaky time off. The kids were enthusiastically practicing what I had told them to do so I put the oldest in charge and told them I'd be back in five minutes. It was worth it. The top floor of the triplex was known as the tower room. It was a simple square window box. Big. Maybe forty by forty feet. Four sides, all window, with a huge shelf all around that you could sit or stand on, with spectacular views. Spain to the east, California to the west, Santa Claus to the north, and Disney World to the south. "Is this cool or what?" Penelope exclaimed with a grandiose sweep of her arm, beaming from ear to ear. It was.

While we were standing on top of the world, Penelope starts in with "Let me tell you something about Mr. Tantrum Thrower." I could say here that I immediately responded, "Don't tell me, I can't keep a secret and you'll end up getting in trouble . . ."—but that would be a lie. Jaye knows, and even though she was sworn to secrecy, I wouldn't be shocked if some of her close friends (and maybe their friends) heard the gossip.

EXPERIENCES THAT SHAPED MY "I'M A DEPENDS TRAINER" PHILOSOPHY

Worked with two of the best trainers in the country—Brian Kilcommons and Matt Margolis.

Invited to join the Rockland County Police Department by sheriff because of my dog Michelle's reputation as a search dog.

After Police Academy, became part-time member of Rockland Sheriff Dept K-9 Search and Rescue unit.

Co-founder of Amigo Search and Rescue K-9 unit.

Showed a dog in Madison Square Garden at Westminster Dog Show.

Trained a dog for an off-Broadway show.

Taught group classes for the Humane Society and Bide-A-Wee in NYC.

Guest speaker at the 2003 Berkshire SAR (Search and Rescue) Conference.

Interviewed by Greta Van Susteren on Fox News regarding search dogs and the runaway bride Jennifer Willbanks.

Appeared on several cable TV shows answering questions.

Did a cable TV show on Bite Prevention Week.

Judge at the annual Martha's Vineyard Agricultural Fair Dog Show.

Several dozen Hug-a-Tree programs in schools, telling kids what to do and what not to do if lost.

ACKNOWLEDGMENTS

First and foremost, thank you to my wife Jaye for not just tolerating, but supporting our family's immersion into the world of dogs. Even though you said on occasion, "Why couldn't you have been a jeweler and brought *that* business home instead of these dogs?"

Next, my heartfelt thanks to Ivan Kronenfeld, who really got me started writing, resulting in my first book *Michelle and Me* about my K-9 search and rescue missions.

Dennis Gaber, thank you so much. Not for being my accountant giving me the hard news every April, but for seriously suggesting that I go back to dog training when I shared my hatred of my job as a stockbroker. My respect for you enabled me to take a hard look at what I was doing and have the courage to change.

Brian Kilcommons, you've been more than a close friend for the last forty-plus years. More than encouraging me to return to the world of dog training, you mentored me and brought me back up to speed. And, dare I say it, when it comes to training, you are one of the very few I consider my equal, if not better? (Nah.)

Nathalie Casthely, for the many, many hours spent on the phone editing with me, thank you for your insight, professionalism, competence, and most importantly, your persona. You're not just good at what you do, you're fun to work with. Thank you for being you!

Susanna Sturgis, I came to you with a mindset that I didn't need editing. Thank you for opening my eyes and doing a great job.

Jeremy Jones, what a stroke of luck that you hired me to help you with your dog. Because now, as my apprentice, you've become much more to me than a competent dog trainer, you're a close friend. Not to mention that lessons are much more fun with a partner.

Jamie Kageleiry (Stringfellow), Executive Editor of the *Martha's Vineyard Times*. Thank you for encouraging me and giving me the column, "Ask the Dog Charmer," in your newspaper. This writing connection has been more than fun, it's been a tremendously valuable asset in the writing of this book.

Thanks to Holly Nadler, a writer herself, for introducing me to Jamie Stringfellow.

A special thanks to Nicole Mele and Skyhorse Publishing for having the faith to publish what I have to say.

Finally, thank you to all my dogs over the years: Cheeta-Ann, pharaoh hound (best dog ever with babies and kids), Michelle and Mike, Dobes (great search dogs—Michelle found two people alive, and Mike tracked a woman eleven miles), Tri, Cavalier King Charles spaniel (as sweet, fun, and gentle as a dog can be) (and Jaye's favorite), MacDuff, mini pin (as a pushy five and a half pounder you were a pleasure to put in a pocket and take everywhere), and, finally, Paula Jean, standard poodle (we adopted you four years ago at age two, and you're smarter and more fun than some of my friends). Thank you all for keeping me so connected to the world of dogs.